# A Brief History of Artificial Intelligence

What It Is, Where We Are,
and Where We Are Going

Michael Wooldridge

FLATIRON
BOOKS
NEW YORK

www.flatironbooks.com

Designed by Jonathan Bennett

Library of Congress Cataloging-in-Publication Data

Names: Wooldridge, Michael J., 1966– author.
Title: A brief history of artificial intelligence : what it is, where we are, and
    where we are going / Michael Wooldridge.
Other titles: Road to conscious machines
Description: First U.S. edition. | New York : Flatiron Books, 2021.
Identifiers: LCCN 2020048545 | ISBN 9781250770745 (hardcover) |
    ISBN 9781250770738 (ebook)
Subjects: LCSH: Artificial intelligence—History.
Classification: LCC Q335 .W658 2021 | DDC 006.3—dc23
LC record available at https://lccn.loc.gov/2020048545

Our books may be purchased in bulk for promotional, educational, or business use. Please contact your local bookseller or the Macmillan Corporate and Premium Sales Department at 1-800-221-7945, extension 5442, or by email at MacmillanSpecialMarkets@macmillan.com.

Originally published in Great Britain in 2020 as *The Road to Conscious Machines* by Pelican, an imprint of Penguin Books UK

First U.S. Edition: 2021

10  9  8  7  6  5  4  3  2

# A Brief History of Artificial Intelligence

*For Janine, Lily, and Tom*

# Contents

# Introduction

ABOUT HALFWAY THROUGH writing this book, I was having lunch with a colleague.

"What are you working on?" she asked me.

This is a standard question for academics—we ask it of each other all the time. I should have been ready for it and had an impressive answer ready at hand.

"Something a bit different. I'm writing a popular science introduction to artificial intelligence."

She snorted. "Does the world really need yet another popular science introduction to AI? What's the main idea, then? What's your new angle?"

I was crestfallen. I needed a clever comeback. So I made a joke.

"It's the story of AI through failed ideas."

She looked at me, her smile now faded. "It's going to be a bloody long book, then."

* * *

Artificial intelligence (AI) is my life. I fell in love with AI as a student in the mid-1980s, and I remain passionate about it today. I love AI, not because I think it will make me rich (although that would be nice) nor because I believe it will transform our world (although, as we will see in this book, I believe it *will* do so in many important ways). I love AI because it is the most endlessly fascinating subject I know of. It draws upon and contributes to an astonishing range of disciplines, including philosophy, psychology, cognitive science, neuroscience, logic, statistics, economics, and robotics. And ultimately, of course, AI appeals to fundamental questions about the human condition and our status as *Homo sapiens*—what it means to be human, and whether humans are unique.

## WHAT AI IS (AND ISN'T)

My first main goal in this book is to tell you what AI is—and, perhaps more important, what it is not. You might find this a little surprising, because it may seem obvious to you what AI is all about. Surely, the long-term dream of AI is to build machines that have the full range of capabilities for intelligent action that people have—to build machines that are self-aware, conscious, and autonomous in the same way that people like you and me are. You will probably have encountered this version of the AI dream in science fiction movies, TV shows, and books.

This version of AI may seem intuitive and obvious, but as we will see when we try to understand what it really means, we encounter many difficulties. The truth is we don't remotely understand what it is we want to create or the mechanisms that create it in people. Moreover, it is by no means the case that there is agreement that this really *is* the goal of AI. In fact, it is fiercely contentious—there isn't even any consensus that this kind of AI is feasible, let alone desirable.

For these reasons, this version of AI—*the grand dream*—is

difficult to approach directly, and although it makes for great books, movies, and video games, it isn't in the mainstream of AI research. Of course, the grand dream raises quite profound philosophical questions—and we will discuss many of these in this book. But beyond these, much of what is written about this version of AI is really nothing more than speculation. Some of it is of the lunatic fringe variety—AI has always attracted crackpots, charlatans, and snake oil salesmen as well as brilliant scientists.

Nevertheless, the public debate on AI, and the seemingly never-ending press fascination with it, is largely fixated on the grand dream and on alarmist dystopian scenarios that have become a weary trope when reporting on AI (AI will take all our jobs; AI will get smarter than we are, and then it will be out of control; superintelligent AI might go wrong and eliminate humanity). Much of what is published about AI in the popular press is ill-informed or irrelevant. Most of it is garbage, from a technical point of view, however entertaining it might be.

In this book, I want to change that narrative. I want to tell you about what AI *actually* is, what AI researchers *actually* work on, and *how they go about it*. The reality of AI for the foreseeable future is very different from the grand dream. It is perhaps less immediately attention grabbing, but it is, as I will show in this book, tremendously exciting in its own right. The mainstream of AI research today is focused around getting machines to do specific tasks that currently require human brains (and also, potentially, human bodies) and for which conventional computing techniques provide no solution. This century has witnessed important advances in this area, which is why AI is so fêted at present. Automated translation tools are one example of an AI technology that was firmly in the realm of science fiction twenty years ago, which has become a practical, everyday reality within the past decade. Such tools have many limitations, but they are successfully used by millions of people across the globe every day. Within the next decade, we will see high-quality real-time spoken-word language translation and augmented reality tools that will change the way we perceive, understand, and relate to the world we live in. Driverless cars are a realistic prospect, and AI looks set to have transformative applications in health care, from which we will all stand to benefit: AI systems have proven to be better than people at recognizing abnormalities such as tumors on x-rays and ultrasound scans, and wearable technology, coupled with AI, has the potential to monitor our health on a continual basis, giving us advance warnings of heart disease, stress, and even dementia. *This* is the kind of thing that AI researchers actually work on. *This* is what excites me about AI. And this is what the AI narrative should be about.

To understand what AI today is and why AI is for the most part not concerned with the grand dream, we also need to understand why AI is hard to create. Over the past sixty years, huge amounts of effort (and research funding) have flowed into AI, and yet, sadly, robot butlers are not likely any time soon. So why has AI proved to be so difficult? To understand the answer to this question, we need to understand what computers are and what computers can do, at their most fundamental level. This takes us into the realm of some of the deepest questions in mathematics and the work of one of the greatest minds of the twentieth century: Alan Turing.

## THE STORY OF AI

My second main goal in this book is to tell you the story of AI from its inception. Every story must have a plot, and we are told there are really only seven basic plots for all the stories in existence, so which of these best fits the story of AI? Many of my colleagues would dearly like it to be "Rags to Riches," and it has certainly turned out that way for a clever (or lucky) few.

For reasons that will become clear later, we could also plausibly view the AI story as "Slaying the Beast"—the beast, in this case, being an abstract mathematical theory called *computational complexity*, which came to explain why so many AI problems proved fearsomely hard to solve. "The Quest" would also work, because the story of AI is indeed rather like that of medieval knights on a quest to find the Holy Grail: full of religious fervor, hopeless optimism, false leads, dead ends, and bitter disappointments. But in the end, the plot that best fits AI is "Fall and Rise," because, only twenty years ago, AI was a rather niche area with a somewhat questionable academic reputation—but since then, it has risen to be the most vibrant and celebrated area in contemporary science. It would be more accurate, though, to say that the plot to the AI story is "Rise and Fall and Rise and Fall and Rise." AI has been the subject of continuous research for more than half a century, but during this time, AI researchers have repeatedly claimed to have made breakthroughs that bring the dream of intelligent machines within reach, only to have their claims exposed as hopelessly overoptimistic in every case. As a consequence, AI is notorious for boom-and-bust cycles—there have been at least three such cycles in the past four decades. At several points over the past sixty years, the bust has been so severe that it seemed like AI might never recover—and yet, in each case, it did. If you imagine that science is all about orderly progress from ignorance to enlightenment, then I'm afraid you are in for a bit of a shock.

Right now, we are in boom times yet again, and excitement is at a fever pitch. At such a time of fevered expectations, it is, I think, essential that the troubled story of AI is told and told again. AI researchers have, more than once, thought they had discovered the magic ingredient to propel AI to its destiny—and the breathless, wide-eyed discussion of current AI has precisely the same tone. Sundar Pichai, CEO of Google, was reported to have claimed that "AI is one of the most important things human-ity is working on. It is more profound than, I dunno, electricity or fire."[1] This followed an earlier claim by Andrew Ng, to the effect that AI was "the new electricity."[2] It is important to re-member what came of such hubris in the past. Yes, there have been real advances, and yes, they are cause for celebration and excitement—but they will not take us to the grand dream. As an AI researcher with thirty years of experience, I have learned to be obsessively cautious about the claims made for my field: I have a very well-developed sense of skepticism about claims for breakthroughs. What AI needs now, perhaps more than any-thing, is a very large injection of humility. I am reminded of the story from ancient Rome of the *auriga*—a slave who would ac-company a triumphant general on his victory march through the city, repeatedly whispering in the general's ear the Latin phrase *memento homo*—"Remember, you are only human."

The second part of this book, therefore, tells the story of AI, warts and all, in broadly chronological order. The story of AI begins just after the creation of the first computers follow-ing the Second World War. I will take you through each of the boom periods—starting with the golden age of AI, a pe-riod of unbridled optimism, when it seemed for a while that rapid progress was being made on a broad range of fronts, next through the "knowledge era," when the big idea was to give machines all the knowledge that we have about our world, and, more recently, the behavioral period, which insisted that robots should be center stage in AI, taking us up to the present time—the era of deep learning. In each case, we'll meet the ideas and the people that shaped AI in their time.

## THE FUTURE FOR AI

While I believe it is important to understand the present hub-bub about all things AI within the context of a long history of failed ideas (and to temper one's excitement accordingly), I also believe there is real cause for optimism about AI right now. There *have* been genuine scientific breakthroughs, and these, coupled with the availability of "big data" and very cheap computer power, have made possible in the past decade AI systems that the founders of the field would have hailed as miraculous. So my third main goal is to tell you what AI systems can actually do right now and what they might be able to do soon—and to point out their limitations.

This leads me into a discussion of fears about AI. As I mentioned above, the public debate about AI is dominated by dystopian scenarios such as AI taking over the world. Recent advances in AI *do* raise issues that we should all be concerned about, such as the nature of employment in the age of AI and how AI technologies might affect human rights—but discussions about whether robots will take over the world (or whatever) take the headlines away from these very important and immediate concerns. So once again, I want to change the narrative. I want to take you through the main areas of concern and to signpost as clearly as I can what you *should* be afraid of and what you should not.

Finally, I want us to have some fun. So in the final chapter, we will return to the grand dream of AI—conscious, self-aware, autonomous machines. We will dig into that dream in more detail and ask what it would mean to realize it, what such machines would be like—and whether they would be like us.

## HOW TO READ THIS BOOK

The remainder of this book is structured around these overarching goals: to tell you what AI is and why it is hard; to tell you the story of AI—the ideas and people that drove it through each of its boom periods; and finally, to showcase what AI can do now and what it can't, and to talk a little about the long-term prospects for AI.

One of the pleasures of writing this book has been to cast off the usual important but tiresome conventions of academic writing. Thus, there are relatively few references, although I give citations for the most important points and a couple of recommendations for further reading at the end of the book.

Not only have I avoided giving extensive references, I've also steered clear of technical details—by which I mean *mathematical* details. My hope is that, after reading this book, you will have a broad understanding of the main ideas and concepts that have driven AI throughout its history. Most of these ideas and concepts are, in truth, highly mathematical in nature. But I am acutely aware of Stephen Hawking's dictum that every equation in a book will halve its readership.

Key technical terms in the book are highlighted in **boldface**.

The book is *highly* selective. I really had no choice here: AI is an enormous field, and it would be utterly impossible to do justice to all the different ideas, traditions, and schools of thought that have influenced AI over the past sixty years. Instead, I have tried to single out what I see as being the main threads which make up the complex tapestry that is the story of AI.

Finally, I should caution that this is not a textbook: I am painting a very finely detailed picture with a very broad brush. Reading this book will not equip you with the skills to start a new AI company or to join the staff of DeepMind (the most celebrated AI company of the present era). What you will gain from this book is an understanding of what AI is and where it might be heading. I hope that after reading it, you will be properly informed about the *reality* of AI—and, after reading it, you will help me to change the narrative.

OXFORD, MAY 2019

# 1

## Turing's Electronic Brains

EVERY STORY NEEDS to start somewhere, and for AI, we have many possible choices, because the dream of AI, in some form or other, is an ancient one.

We could choose to begin in classical Greece, with the story of Hephaestus, blacksmith to the gods, who had the power to bring metal creatures to life.

We could begin in the city of Prague in the 1600s, where, according to legend, the head rabbi created the golem—a magical being fashioned from clay, intended to protect the city's Jewish population from anti-Semitic attacks.

We could begin with James Watt in eighteenth-century Scotland, designing the Governor, an ingenious automatic control system for the steam engines he was building, thereby laying the foundations for modern control theory.

We could begin in the early nineteenth century with the young Mary Shelley, cooped up in a Swiss villa during a spell of bad weather, creating the story of Frankenstein to entertain her husband, the poet Percy Bysshe Shelley, and their family friend, the notorious Lord Byron.

We could begin in London in the 1830s with Ada Lovelace, estranged daughter of the same Lord Byron, striking up a friendship with Charles Babbage, curmudgeonly inventor of mechanical calculating machines, and inspiring the brilliant young Ada to speculate about whether machines might ultimately be creative.

We could equally well begin with the eighteenth-century fascination with automata—cunningly designed machines that gave some illusion of life.

We have many possible choices for the beginning of AI, but for me, the beginning of the AI story coincides with the beginning of the story of computing itself, for which we have a pretty clear starting point: King's College, Cambridge, in 1935, and a brilliant but unconventional young student called Alan Turing.

## CAMBRIDGE, 1935

It is hard to imagine now, because he is about as famous as any mathematician could ever hope to be, but until the 1980s, the name of Alan Turing was virtually unknown outside the fields of mathematics and computer science. While students of mathematics and computing might have come across Turing's name in their studies, they would have known little about the full extent of his achievements or his tragic, untimely death. In part, this is because some of Turing's most important work was carried out in secret for the UK government during the Second World War, and the facts of this remarkable work remained classified until the 1970s.[1] But there was surely also prejudice at work here, because Turing was gay at a time when homosexuality was a criminal offense in the United Kingdom. In 1952, he was prosecuted and convicted for what was then called *gross indecency*. His penalty was to take a crude hormone drug that was intended to reduce his sexual desires—a form of "chemical castration." He died, apparently by his own hand, two years later, at the age of just forty-one.[2]

Nowadays, of course, we all know a little of the Turing story, although perhaps not quite as much as we should. The best-known part of the story relates to his code-breaking work at Bletchley Park in the Second World War, made famous in the popular (albeit spectacularly inaccurate) 2014 Hollywood movie *The Imitation Game*. And he certainly deserves enormous credit for that work, which played an important role in the Allied victory. But AI researchers and computer scientists revere him for quite different reasons. He was, for all practical purposes, the inventor of the computer, and shortly after that, he largely invented the field of AI.

Turing was remarkable in many ways, but one of the most remarkable things about him is that he invented computers by accident. As a mathematics student at Cambridge University in the mid-1930s, Turing set himself the precocious challenge of settling one of the leading mathematical problems of the day—a problem that went by the impressive and frankly daunting name of the Entscheidungsproblem. The problem had been posed by the mathematician David Hilbert in 1928. The Entscheidungsproblem asks whether there are mathematical questions that cannot be answered by simply following a recipe. Of course, the questions Hilbert was concerned with were not questions like "Is there a God?" or "What is the meaning of life?" but rather what mathematicians call **decision problems** (*Entscheidungsproblem* is German for "decision problem"). Decision problems are mathematical questions that have a yes/no answer. Here are some examples of decision problems:

- **Is it the case that 2 + 2 = 4?**
- **Is it the case that 4 × 4 = 16?**
- **Is it the case that 7,919 is a prime number?**

As it happens, the answer to all these decision problems is *yes*. I hope you will agree the first two are obvious, but unless you have an unhealthy obsession with prime numbers, you would have had to work a little to answer the last one. So let's think about this final question for a moment.

A prime number, as you will no doubt recall, is a whole number that is only exactly divisible by itself and one. Now, with this in mind, I'm pretty sure you could, at least in principle, find the answer to the final question on your own. There is an obvious method for doing so that is very straightforward, albeit rather tedious for numbers as large as 7,919: check every number that could possibly be a divisor to see whether it divides 7,919 exactly. Follow this procedure carefully, and you will discover that none do: 7,919 is indeed a prime number.[3]

What is important here is that there are precise and unambiguous methods for answering questions like those above. These methods don't require any *intelligence* to apply them—they are nothing more than *recipes*, which can be followed by rote. All we need to do to find the answer is to follow the recipe *precisely*.

Since we have a technique that is guaranteed to answer the question (given sufficient time), we say that questions in the form "Is *n* a prime number?" are **decidable.** I emphasize that all this means is that, whenever we are faced with a question in the form "Is *n* a prime number?" we know that we can definitely find the answer if we are given sufficient time: we follow the relevant recipe, and eventually, we will get the correct answer.

Now, the Entscheidungsproblem asks whether *all* mathematical decision problems like those we saw above are decidable or whether there are some for which there is *no* recipe for finding the answer—no matter how much time you are prepared to put in.

This is a very fundamental question—it asks whether mathematics can be reduced to merely following recipes. And answering this fundamental question was the daunting challenge that Turing set himself in 1935—and which he triumphantly resolved, with dizzying speed.

When we think of deep mathematical problems, we imagine that any solution to them must involve complex equations and long proofs. And sometimes this is indeed the case—when the British mathematician Andrew Wiles famously proved Fermat's last theorem in the early 1990s, it took years for the mathematical community to understand the hundreds of pages of his proof and become confident that it was indeed correct. By these standards, Turing's solution to the Entscheidungsproblem was positively eccentric.

Apart from anything else, Turing's proof is short and comparatively accessible (once the basic framework has been established, the proof is really just a few lines long). But most important, to solve the Entscheidungsproblem, Turing realized that he needed to be able to make the idea of a recipe that can be followed precisely exact. To do this, he invented a mathematical problem-solving machine—nowadays, we call these **Turing machines** in his honor. A Turing machine is a mathematical description of a recipe, like the one for checking prime numbers mentioned above. All a Turing machine does is to follow the recipe it was designed for. I should emphasize that, although Turing called them *machines,* at this point they were nothing more than an abstract mathematical idea. The idea of solving a deep mathematical problem by *inventing a machine* was unconventional, to say the least—I suspect many mathematicians of the day were mystified.

Turing machines are very powerful beasts. Any kind of mathematical recipe that you might care to think of can be encoded as a Turing machine. And if all mathematical decision problems can be solved by following a recipe, then for any decision problem, you should be able to design a Turing machine to solve it. To settle Hilbert's problem, all you had to do was show that there was some decision problem that could not be answered by any Turing machine. And that is what Turing did.

His next trick was to show that his machines could be turned into *general-purpose* problem-solving machines. He designed a Turing machine that will follow *any* recipe that you give it. We now call these general-purpose Turing machines **universal Turing machines:**[4] and a computer, when stripped down to its bare essentials, is simply a universal Turing machine made real. The programs that a computer runs are just recipes, like the one for prime numbers that we discussed above.

Although it isn't central to our story, it is worth at least mentioning how Turing settled the Entscheidungsproblem using his new invention—apart from the fact that it was extraordinarily ingenious, it also has some bearing on the question of whether AI is ultimately possible.

His idea was that Turing machines could be programmed to *answer questions about other Turing machines.* He considered the following decision problem: given a Turing machine and an associated input, will it be guaranteed to eventually halt with an answer, or could it carry on doing its work forever? This is a decision problem of the type that we discussed above—albeit a much more involved one. Now, suppose there was a machine that could solve this problem. Turing saw that the existence of a Turing machine that could answer this question would create a contradiction. It followed that there could be no recipe for checking whether a Turing machine halts, and so the question "Does a Turing machine halt?" is an **undecidable problem.** He had thus established that there are decision problems that cannot be solved by simply following a recipe. He thereby settled Hilbert's Entscheidungsproblem: mathematics could not be reduced to following recipes. In fact, he was almost scooped by a Princeton mathematician by the name of Alonzo Church, but Turing's proof is very different from that of Church: much more direct and much more general. And a by-product of Turing's proof was the invention of the universal Turing machine—a general-purpose problem-solving machine. Turing didn't invent his machines with the idea of actually building them, but the idea occurred to him soon enough, and many others too. In wartime Munich, Konrad Zuse designed a computer called the Z3 for the Reich Air Ministry—although it was not quite a modern computer, it introduced many of the key ingredients of one. Across the Atlantic in Pennsylvania, a team led by John Mauchly and J. Presper Eckert developed a machine called ENIAC to compute artillery tables. With some tweaks by the brilliant Hungarian mathematician John von Neumann, ENIAC established the fundamental architecture of the modern computer (the architecture of conventional computers is called the Von Neumann architecture, in his honor). Over in postwar England, Fred Williams and Tom Kilburn built the Manchester Baby, which led directly to the world's first commercial computer, the Ferranti Mark 1—Turing himself joined the staff of Manchester University in 1948 and wrote some of the first programs to run on it.

By the 1950s, all the key ingredients of the modern computer had been developed. Machines that realized Turing's mathematical vision were a practical reality—all you needed was enough money to buy one and a building big enough (to house the Ferranti Mark 1 required two storage bays, each sixteen feet long, eight feet high, and four feet wide; the machine consumed twenty-seven kilowatts of electricity—about enough to power three modern homes). Of course, they have been getting smaller and cheaper ever since.

## WHAT ELECTRONIC BRAINS ACTUALLY DO

Nothing pleases a newspaper editor more than a catchy headline, and when the first computers were built after the Second

World War, newspapers across the world heralded the arrival of a miraculous new invention—*the electronic brain.* These fearsomely complex machines were apparently capable of dazzling feats of mathematics, for example, processing huge volumes of convoluted arithmetic problems much faster and more accurately than any human could ever dream of doing. To those unacquainted with the realities of computers, it must have seemed that machines capable of such tasks must be gifted with some kind of superior intelligence. *Electronic brain* therefore seemed like an obvious label, and it stuck. (One still came across this kind of language as late as the early 1980s, when I first became interested in computers.) In fact, it turns out that what these electronic brains were doing was something incredibly useful—and something that people find tremendously difficult—but not something that requires *intelligence.* And understanding exactly what computers are designed to do—and what they can't do—is central to understanding AI and why it is so difficult.

Remember that Turing machines and their physical manifestation in the form of computers are nothing more than *machines for following instructions.* That is their sole purpose—that is all they are designed to do and all they can do. The instructions that we give a Turing machine are what we nowadays call an *algorithm* or *program.*[5] Most programmers are probably not even aware of the fact that they are interacting with what amounts to a Turing machine, and for good reason—programming Turing machines directly is incredibly fiddly and irksome, as generations of frustrated computer science students would confirm. Instead, we build higher-level languages on top of the Turing machines, to make it simpler to program them—programming languages like Python, Java, and C. All these languages really do is hide some of the gory details of the machine from the programmer in order to make it a bit more accessible. But they are still incredibly fiddly and irksome, which is why programming is hard, why computer programs crash so often, and why good programmers get paid so much.

I have no intention of trying to teach you to program, but it is useful to have some sense of what kinds of instructions computers can follow. Roughly speaking, all a computer can do is follow lists of instructions such as the following:[6]

- **Add A to B**

- **If the result is bigger than C, then do D; otherwise, do E**

- **Repeatedly do F until G**

*Every* computer program boils down to lists of instructions similar to these. Microsoft Word and PowerPoint boil down to instructions like these. *Call of Duty* and *Minecraft* boil down to instructions like these. Facebook, Google, and eBay boil down to instructions like these. The apps on your smartphone, from your web browser to Tinder, all boil down to instructions like these. *And if we are to build intelligent machines, then their intelligence must ultimately reduce to simple, explicit instructions like these.* This, in essence, is the fundamental challenge of AI. The question of whether AI is possible ultimately amounts to whether we can produce intelligent behavior simply by following lists of instructions like these.

In the remainder of this chapter, I want to dig into this observation and try to make explicit some of the implications it has for AI. Before I do this, however, in case it seems like I'm trying to convince you that computers are actually rather useless beasts, I feel obliged to point out several features that make computers rather more useful than they might at this stage appear.

The first point to make is that computers are *fast*. Very, very, very fast. Of course, you know this—but our experiences in the everyday world do not really equip us to understand quite

how fast computers actually are. So let us quantify this statement. At the time of writing, a reasonable desktop computer
operating at full speed can carry out up to *one hundred billion
instructions of the type listed above every second*. One hundred billion is approximately the number of stars in our galaxy, but that
probably doesn't help much. So let me put it this way. Suppose
you wanted to emulate the computer, by manually carrying out
the computer's instructions yourself. Imagine you carry out
one instruction every ten seconds and that you don't pause for
breaks—you work twenty-four/seven/three-sixty-five to get the
job done. Then it would take you about *3,700 years* to do what
the computer does in *just one second*.

Of course, as well as being *much* slower as a machine for following recipes, you are different from a computer in one other
key respect: there is just no way that you could spend a serious amount of time following instructions in this way without making mistakes. Computers, by contrast, very rarely make
mistakes. While programs frequently crash, these crashes are
almost invariably the fault of the people who wrote the program rather than a fault in the computer itself. Modern computer processors are phenomenally reliable—they are expected
to operate on average for up to fifty thousand hours before failing, faithfully carrying out tens of billions of instructions for
every second of those hours.

One final observation. Although computers are just machines for following instructions, this does not mean that
they are incapable of making decisions. Computers certainly
*can* make decisions—it is just that we have to give them precise instructions about *how* to make the decision. And a computer can subsequently adjust these instructions for itself, as
long as we have instructed it how to do so—in this way, as
we will see, a computer can change its behavior over time—it
can *learn*.

## WHY IS AI HARD?

Computers, then, can *reliably* follow *very simple* instructions *very, very quickly,* and they can *make decisions* as long as those decisions are precisely specified. Now, some things that we might want computers to do for us are very easy to encode in this way—but others are not. To understand why AI is hard— why progress has proved so elusive over the years—it helps to look at problems that are easy to encode in this way and problems that are not, and to see why this is the case. Figure 1 displays some tasks that we might want computers to do and shows how difficult it has proved to get computers to achieve them.

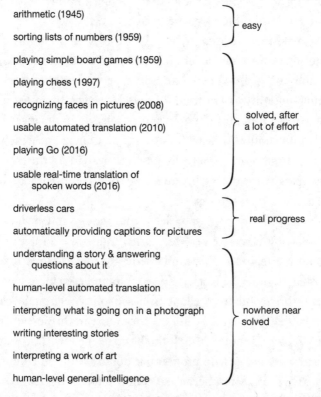

**Figure 1:** Some tasks that we want computers to be able to do ranked in order of difficulty. Years in parentheses indicate approximately when the problem was solved. At present, we have no idea about how to get computers to do the tasks at the bottom of the list.

At the top is arithmetic. It was very easy to get computers to do arithmetic, because all the basic arithmetical operations (addition, subtraction, multiplication, division) can be carried out by a simple recipe—you were taught such recipes at school, even if you don't recall them now. These recipes can be directly translated into computer programs, and so problems involving the straightforward application of arithmetic were solved in the very earliest days of computing. (The first program Turing wrote for the Manchester Baby computer when he joined the staff of Manchester University was to carry out long division—it must have been an odd experience for Turing, returning to basic arithmetic after solving one of the deepest mathematical problems of the twentieth century.)

Next we have sorting, by which I just mean arranging a list of numbers into, say, ascending order or a list of names into alphabetical order. There are some very simple recipes for sorting—see if you can think of one. However, the most obvious of these are painfully slow and not usable in practice: 1959 saw the invention of a technique called Quicksort, which for the first time provided a really practical way to do this. (In the sixty years since it was invented, nobody has managed to do much better than Quicksort.[7])

Then we move on to problems that require much more effort. Playing board games well turned out to be a major challenge, for a reason that is fundamental to the AI story. It turns out that there is in fact a very simple and elegant recipe for playing board games well; it is based on a technique called **search,** about which we will hear a lot more in the next chapter. The problem is that although the basic recipe for game playing by search is very easy to program, it doesn't work on all but the most trivial of games, because it requires too much time or too much computer memory—even if we could use every atom in the universe to build a computer, that computer would not be remotely powerful enough to be able to play chess or Go using "naive" search. To make search viable, we need something extra—and as we will see in the next chapter, this is where AI comes in.

This situation—we know how to solve a problem in principle, but these techniques don't work in practice because they would require impossibly large amounts of computing resources—is extremely common in AI, and a huge body of research has grown up around dealing with it.

The next problems on the list, though, are very much not of this type. Recognizing faces in a picture, automated translation, and usable real-time translation of spoken words are all very different kinds of problems because, unlike board games, conventional computing techniques give us no clues about how to write a recipe to solve them. We need a completely new approach. In each of these cases, though, the problem has been solved, by a technique called *machine learning*, about which we will hear a lot more later on in this book.

Next, we move on to driverless cars. This problem is fascinating because it is something that seems so straightforward for people to do. We don't associate the ability to drive a car with *intelligence*. But it turned out to be fearsomely hard to get computers to drive cars. The main problem is that a car needs to understand where it is and what is going on around it. Imagine a driverless car at a busy road intersection in New York City. There will probably be many vehicles in continual movement, with pedestrians, cyclists, construction, traffic signs, and road markings in the picture as well. It may be raining or snowing or foggy, just to complicate things further (and in New York, it may well be all three at the same time). In situations like this, the main difficulty is not *deciding what to do* (slow down, speed up, turn left, turn right, etc.) but rather *making sense of what is going on around you*—identifying where you are, what vehicles are present, where they are and what they are doing, where the pedestrians are, and so on. If you have all that information, then deciding what you need to do is usually going to be pretty easy. (We will discuss the specific challenges of driverless cars later in the book.)

Then we move on to problems that we really have little idea how to solve. How can a computer understand a complex story and answer questions about it? How can a computer translate a rich, nuanced text such as a novel? How can a computer interpret what is going on in a picture—not just identifying the people in it, but *actually interpreting what is going on*? How can a computer write an interesting story or interpret a work of art such as a painting? And the final one—the grand dream of computers with general-purpose human-level intelligence—is the greatest of all.

Progress in AI, then, means progressively getting computers to do more and more of these tasks in figure 1. Those that are difficult are so for usually one of two reasons. The first possibility is that while we do in fact have a recipe for the problem that works *in principle*, it doesn't work *in practice* because it would require impossibly large amounts of computing time and memory. Board games like chess and Go fall into this category. The second possibility is that we just have no real idea what a recipe for solving the problem might look like (e.g., recognizing faces), in which latter case we would need something completely new (e.g., machine learning). Pretty much all of contemporary AI is concerned with problems that fall into one of these two categories.

Let's now turn to the hardest problem in figure 1—the grand dream of general-purpose, human-level intelligence. Not surprisingly, this challenge has attracted a lot of attention, and one of the earliest and most influential thinkers on the subject was our old friend Alan Turing.

## THE TURING TEST

The development of the first computers in the late 1940s and early 1950s prompted a flurry of public debate about the potential of these wondrous feats of modern science. One of the highest-profile contributions to the debate at the time was a book entitled *Cybernetics,* written by an MIT mathematics professor called Norbert Wiener. The book made explicit parallels between machines and animal brains and nervous systems, and touched on many ideas relating to AI. It attracted huge public interest, despite the fact that it was surely incomprehensible to any but the most dedicated and mathematically adept reader. Questions such as whether machines could "think" began to be seriously debated in the press and on radio shows (in 1951, Turing himself participated in a BBC radio show on this very subject). Although it didn't yet have a name, the idea of AI was in the air.

Prompted by the public debate, Turing began to think seriously about the possibility of artificial intelligence. He was particularly irritated with claims being made in the public debate along the lines of "Machines will never be able to do *x*" (where *x* is, for example, think, reason, or be creative). He wanted to definitively silence those who argued that "machines cannot think." To this end, he proposed a test, which we now call the **Turing test.** Turing's test has been hugely influential since he first described it in 1950, and it is still the subject of serious research to the present day. Sadly, though, for reasons that will become clear later, it failed to silence the doubters.

Turing's inspiration was a Victorian-era parlor game called the Imitation Game. The basic idea of the Imitation Game was for someone to try to tell if another person was a man or a woman simply on the basis of the answers they gave to questions that were posed to them. Turing proposed that you could use a similar test for AI. The way the test is usually described is something like this:

Human interrogators interact via a computer keyboard and screen with something that is either a person or a computer program—the interrogator does not know in advance whether it is a person or a program. The interaction is purely in the form of textual questions and answers: the interrogator types a question, and a response is displayed. The task of the interrogator is to determine whether the thing being interrogated is a person or a computer program.

Now, suppose that the thing being interrogated is indeed a computer program, but after some reasonable amount of time, the interrogators cannot reliably tell whether they are interacting with a program or a person. Then surely, Turing argued, you should accept that the program has some sort of human-level intelligence (or whatever you want to call it).

Turing's brilliant move here is to sidestep all the questions and debate whether a program was "really" intelligent (or conscious or whatever). Whether or not the program is "really" thinking (or is conscious or self-aware or whatever) is irrelevant because it is doing something that makes it *indistinguishable from the "real thing."* The key word here is *indistinguishable.*

The Turing test is a neat example of a standard technique in science. If you want to find out whether two things are the same or different, ask whether there is some reasonable test you can apply that would distinguish them. If there is a reasonable test that one would pass but the other would not, then you can be confident that they are different. If you can't distinguish them by any such test, then you can't claim they are different. Turing's test is concerned with distinguishing machine intelligence from human intelligence, and the test is whether a person can distinguish the behavior that each produces.

Notice that the only evidence that the interrogators have to go on are the inputs and outputs—the questions sent by the interrogator and the responses that the interrogator later receives. The thing they are interrogating is a *black box* as far as the Turing test is concerned, in the sense that we are not allowed to examine its internal structure: all that we have are the inputs and outputs. This is important, because it means the Turing test cannot take into account *how* the entity being tested actually works—only the behavior it produces.

Turing's article "Computing Machinery and Intelligence," describing his test, was published in the prestigious international journal *Mind* in 1950.[8] Although many articles touching on AI-like ideas had been published before this, Turing approached the subject for the first time from the standpoint of the modern digital computer. As such, his article is generally recognized as the first AI publication.

## TURING TEST NONSENSE

The Turing test is simple, elegant, and easy to understand. However, it had the unfortunate side effect of establishing the test as the holy grail of AI—with unfortunate consequences that resonate to the present day.

The problem is that most attempts to tackle the Turing test tend to use cheap tricks to try to befuddle the interrogators into believing that they are dealing with human intelligence rather than by trying to seriously engage with the actual issues of intelligent behavior. The most famous example of this was a program called **ELIZA,** written by the German American MIT computer scientist Joseph Weizenbaum in the mid-1960s. ELIZA was never intended by Weizenbaum to be a contender for the Turing test—it was a serious and influential scientific experiment in its own right—but sadly, it has since become synonymous with superficial approaches to AI generally and the Turing test in particular.

ELIZA takes the role of a psychiatrist talking to a patient,

asking open-ended questions to get the interviewee to contemplate themselves. ELIZA worked by picking up on key words
like *family, friends, lonely, sad,* and so on and then used canned
scripts associated with the relevant word to issue follow-up
questions. You don't have to be very perceptive to see beyond its
smoke and mirrors. Here is a dialogue with a modern version of
the system (ELIZA responses are in italics):

> I am lonely.
>
> *Are you lonely often?*
>
> Yes. Almost every day.
>
> *Why do you say almost every day?*
>
> I think it is my family.
>
> *Tell me something about your family.*
>
> They hate me.
>
> *What makes you believe they hate you?*
>
> They are mean to me.
>
> *Earlier you said you felt lonely?*
>
> What is the meaning of life?
>
> *Maybe your life has something to do with this.*
>
> What is the purpose of existence?
>
> *Is it because of your plans that you say what is the purpose of existence?*

The opening is promising enough, but even after a couple of
sentences, the superficiality of the interaction becomes painfully
clear—ELIZA obviously has no understanding of the dialogue
(and of course Weizenbaum never claimed that it did—that
was not the point of his experiment).

Weizenbaum could hardly have anticipated the impact that
ELIZA would have, both within academia and beyond. He
was, apparently, startled to discover that users took his simple

experiment seriously. It immediately entered the folklore of AI. I remember as a Ph.D. student in the 1980s hearing that lonely and socially ill-adjusted graduate students would converse all night with ELIZA, as a proxy for the human relationships they were incapable of forming; there was even a story—hopefully apocryphal—about ELIZA unwittingly encouraging a depressed student to commit suicide.

ELIZA's legacy lives on to this day, in the form of the annual Loebner Prize competition. It isn't clear whether Turing imagined that anyone would ever actually try out his test for real, but, in 1990, that is precisely what American millionaire inventor Hugh Loebner decided to do. Every year, the Loebner Prize invites the submission of computer programs to engage in the Turing test, attempting to convince a panel of judges that they are in fact people. A successful entry stands to win $100,000.

Loebner's competition was instantly controversial—famous AI scientist Marvin Minsky dismissed it as a "meaningless publicity stunt." The competition seems to generate at least one hopelessly misleading headline every year. The problem is that entries in the Loebner competition are, for the most part, variations on the ELIZA theme. Rather than trying to win by engaging the interrogators in a meaningful conversation that demonstrates human-level comprehension, common sense, and understanding, they use tricks to misdirect and mislead.

ELIZA is the direct ancestor of a phenomenon that makes AI researchers groan whenever it is mentioned: the internet chatbot. These are internet-based programs that attempt to engage users in conversation, often via social media platforms such as Twitter. Most internet chatbots use nothing more than keyword-based canned scripts in the same way that ELIZA did, and as a consequence, the conversations they produce are every bit as superficial and uninteresting. Chatbots of this kind are not AI.

## VARIETIES OF ARTIFICIAL INTELLIGENCE

For all the nonsense it has given rise to, the Turing test is an important part of the AI story because, for the first time, it gave researchers interested in this emerging discipline a target to aim at. When someone asked you what your goal was, you could give a straightforward and precise answer: *My goal is to build a machine that can meaningfully pass the Turing test.* Today, I think very few, if any, serious AI researchers would give this answer, but it had a crucial historical role, and I believe it still has something important to tell us today.

Much of the attraction of the Turing test undoubtedly lies in its simplicity, but clear as the test appears to be, it nevertheless raises many problematic questions about AI.

Imagine that you are an interrogator in the Turing test. The answers you receive in the test convince you that you are not interacting with a chatbot: whatever is on the other end is demonstrating the kind of understanding of your questions and producing the kinds of answers that a human might demonstrate. It subsequently transpires that the thing on the other end is in fact a computer program. Now, as far as the Turing test is concerned, the matter is settled. The program is doing something indistinguishable from human behavior: end of debate. But there are still at least two logically distinct possibilities:

**1.** The program *actually understands* the dialogue, in much the same sense that a person does.

**2.** The program does not understand, but can *simulate* such understanding.

The first claim—that the program *really does understand*—is much stronger than the second. I suspect most AI researchers— and probably most readers of this book—would accept that programs of type 2 are feasible, at least in principle, but would need a lot more convincing before they accepted that programs of type 1 are. And indeed, it is not obvious how we could substantiate a claim that a program was of type 1—this is not what the Turing test claims to do. (Turing, I suspect, would have been irritated by the distinction: he would have pointed out that one of the main reasons he invented the test was to put an end to arguments about such distinctions.) Aiming to build a program of type 1 is therefore a much more ambitious and controversial goal than building a program of type 2.

The goal of building programs *that really do have understanding (consciousness, etc.) in the way that people do* is called **strong AI;** the weaker goal, of building programs that demonstrate the same capability but without any claim that they *actually possess these attributes,* is called **weak AI.**

## BEYOND THE TURING TEST

There are many variations of Turing's indistinguishability test. For example, in a much stronger version of the test, we can imagine robots that attempt to pass themselves off as people in the everyday world. Here, "indistinguishability" is interpreted in a very demanding way—it means that the machines are indistinguishable from people. (I'm assuming that you aren't allowed to dissect them, so the test is still a sort of black box.) For the foreseeable future, this sort of thing is firmly in the realms of fiction. Indeed, a world where robots were hard to distinguish from people was the basis for at least one very good film, Ridley Scott's 1982 classic, *Blade Runner,* in which Rick Deckard, portrayed by a young Harrison Ford, spends his days carrying out cryptic tests with the aim of determining whether what appears to be a beautiful woman is in fact a robot. Similar themes are explored in movies such as *Ex Machina* (2014).

Although *Blade Runner* scenarios are not in prospect, researchers have begun to ask whether there are variations of the

Turing test that might meaningfully test for genuine intelligence and are resistant to trickery of the chatbot variety. One very simple idea is to test for *comprehension,* and one manifestation of this idea is the use of what are called **Winograd schemas.** These are short questions, perhaps best illustrated by examples:[9]

> **Statement 1a:** The city councilors refused the demonstrators a permit because they <u>feared</u> violence.
>
> **Statement 1b:** The city councilors refused the demonstrators a permit because they <u>advocated</u> violence.
>
> **Question:** Who [feared/advocated] violence?

Notice that these two statements differ from each other in just one word (underlined in each case), but that small change dramatically alters their meaning. The point of the test is to identify who "they" refers to in each case. In Statement 1a, "they" clearly refers to the councilors (they are the ones that fear violence from the demonstrators), while in Statement 1b, "they" refers to the demonstrators (the councilors are concerned about the fact that the demonstrators are advocating violence).

Here is another example:

> **Statement 2a:** The trophy doesn't fit into the brown suitcase because it is too <u>small</u>.
>
> **Statement 2b:** The trophy doesn't fit into the brown suitcase because it is too <u>large</u>.
>
> **Question:** What is too [small/large]?

Obviously, in Statement 2a, the suitcase is too small; in statement 2b, the trophy is too large.

Now, most literate adults would easily be able to handle these examples and others like them—but they resist the kind of cheap tricks used by chatbots. To be able to give the correct answer, it is hard to avoid the conclusion that you really need to *understand* the text and to have some *knowledge* about the kind of scenario in question. To understand the difference between Statements 1a and 1b, for example, you would need to know something about demonstrations (demonstrations often lead to violence) and councilors (that they have the power to grant or deny permits for demonstrations to take place and that they will try to avoid situations that lead to violence).

Another similar challenge for AI involves understanding of the human world and the unwritten rules that govern our relationships within it. Consider the following short dialogue, due to the psychologist and linguist Steven Pinker:

> Bob: I'm leaving you.
>
> Alice: Who is she?

Can you explain this dialogue? Of course you can. It's a staple of TV soap operas: Alice and Bob are in a relationship, and Bob's announcement leads Alice to believe that Bob is leaving her for another woman—and she wants to know who the other woman is. We might also speculate that Alice is pretty angry.

But how could a computer be programmed to understand such dialogues? Such a capability would surely be essential for understanding stories and indeed for writing them. This common-sense, everyday ability to understand the workings of human beliefs, desires, and relationships would be an essential requirement for a computer program capable of following *Days of Our Lives*. We all have this capability, and it would also seem to be a key requirement for both strong and weak AI. But the ability for machines to comprehend and answer questions about such scenarios remains a long way off.

## GENERAL AI

While the grand dream of AI seems intuitively obvious, as we have demonstrated, it is surprisingly hard to define what it means or when we will know that we have found it. For this reason, although strong AI is an important and fascinating part of the AI story, it is largely irrelevant to contemporary AI research. Go to a contemporary AI conference, and you will hear almost nothing about it—except possibly late at night, in the bar.

A lesser goal is to build machines that have general-purpose human-level intelligence. Nowadays, this is usually referred to as **artificial general intelligence (AGI)** or just **general AI. AGI** roughly equates to having a computer that has the full range of intellectual capabilities that a person has—this would include the ability to converse in natural language (cf. the Turing test), solve problems, reason, perceive its environment, and so on, at or above the same level as a typical person. The literature on AGI usually isn't concerned with issues such as consciousness or self-awareness, so AGI might be thought of as a weaker version of weak AI.[10]

However, even this lesser goal is somewhat on the margins of contemporary AI. Instead, what AI researchers usually focus on is building computer programs that can carry out tasks that currently require brains—progressively moving through the list of problems that we saw in figure 1. This approach to AI—getting computers to do very specific tasks—is sometimes called **narrow AI,** but I have rarely heard this term used within the AI community. We don't refer to what we do as narrow AI—because narrow AI *is* AI. This might be disappointing to those of us that long for robot butlers, though it will perhaps be welcome news to those that have nightmares about the robot uprising.

So now you know what AI is and have some idea about why it's hard to achieve. But how, exactly, do AI researchers go about it?

## BRAIN OR MIND?

How might we go about producing human-level intelligent behavior in a computer? Historically, AI has adopted one of two main approaches to this problem. Put crudely, the first possibility involves trying to model *the mind*: the processes of conscious reasoning, problem solving, and so on, which we all make use of as we go about our lives. This approach is called **symbolic AI,** because it makes use of symbols that stand for things that the system is reasoning about. For example, a symbol "room451" within a robot's control system might be the name that the robot uses for your bedroom, and a symbol "cleanRoom" might be used as the name for the activity of cleaning a room. As the robot figures out what to do, it makes explicit use of these symbols, and so, for example, if the robot decides to carry out the action "cleanRoom(room451)," then this means that the robot has decided to clean your bedroom. The symbols the robot is using *mean something* in the robot's environment.

For about thirty years, from the mid-1950s until the late 1980s, symbolic AI was the most widely adopted approach to building AI systems. It has a lot of advantages, but perhaps the most important of these is that it is *transparent:* when the robot concludes that it will "cleanRoom(room451)," then we can immediately understand what it has decided to do. But also, I think it was popular because it seems to reflect our conscious thought processes. We think in terms of symbols—words—and when deciding what to do, we might have a mental conversation with ourselves about the pros and cons of various courses of action. Symbolic AI aspired to capture all this. As we will see in chapter 3, symbolic AI peaked in the early 1980s.

The alternative to modeling the mind is to model the *brain.* One extreme possibility would be to try to simulate a complete human brain (and perhaps a human nervous system) within a computer. After all, human brains are the only things that we can say with certainty are capable of producing human-level intelligent behavior. The problem with this approach is that the brain is an unimaginably complex organ: a human brain contains about one hundred billion interconnected components, and we don't remotely understand the structure and operation of these well enough to duplicate it. It isn't a realistic possibility any time soon, and I suspect it is unlikely ever to be possible (although I'm sorry to say that hasn't stopped some people from trying).[11]

What we can do instead, however, is to take inspiration from some structures that occur in the brain and model these as components in intelligent systems. This research area is called **neural networks,** or **neural nets**—the name comes from the cellular information processing units called *neurons* that we find in the microstructure of the brain. The study of neural nets goes back to before the emergence of AI itself and has evolved alongside the mainstream of AI. It is this area that has shown impressive progress this century, which has led to the current boom in AI.

Symbolic AI and neural nets are very different approaches, with utterly different methodologies. Both have moved in and out of fashion over the past sixty years, and as we will see, there has even been acrimony between the two schools. However, as AI emerged as a new scientific discipline in the 1950s, it was symbolic AI that largely held sway.

# 2

## The Golden Age

ALTHOUGH TURING'S ARTICLE "Computing Machinery and Intelligence," which introduced the Turing test, made what we now recognize as the first substantial scientific contribution to the discipline of AI, it was a rather isolated contribution, because AI as a discipline simply did not exist at the time. It did not have a name, there was no community of researchers working on it, and the only contributions at the time were speculative conceptual ones, such as the Turing test—there were no AI systems. Just a decade later, by the end of the 1950s, all that had changed: a new discipline had been established, with a distinctive name, and researchers were able to proudly show off the first tentative systems demonstrating rudimentary components of intelligent behavior.

The next two decades were the first boom in AI. There was a flush of optimism, growth, and apparent progress, leading to the era called the **golden age of AI,** from about 1956 to 1974. There had been no disappointments yet; everything seemed possible. The AI systems built in this period are legends in the AI canon. Systems with quirky, geeky names like SHRDLU,

STRIPS, and SHAKEY—short names, all in uppercase, supposedly because those were the constraints of computer file names at the time (the tradition of naming AI systems in this way continues to the present day, although it has long since ceased to be necessary). The computers used to build these systems were, by modern standards, unimaginably limited, painfully slow, and tremendously hard to use. The tools we take for granted when developing software today did not exist then and indeed could not have run on the computers of the time. Much of the "hacker" culture of computer programming seems to have emerged at the time. AI researchers worked at night because then they could get access to the computers that were used for more important work during normal office hours; and they had to invent all sorts of ingenious programming tricks to get their complicated programs to run at all—many of these tricks subsequently became standard techniques, with their origins in the AI labs of the 1960s and 1970s now only dimly remembered, if at all.[1]

But by the mid-1970s, progress on AI stalled, having failed to progress far beyond the earliest simple experiments. The young discipline came close to being snuffed out by research funders and a scientific community that came to believe AI, which had promised so much, was actually going nowhere.

In this chapter, we'll look at these first two decades of AI. We'll look at some of the key systems built during this period and discuss one of the most important techniques developed in AI at the time—a technique called a *search*, which to the present day remains a central component of many AI systems. We'll also hear how an abstract mathematical theory called *computational complexity*, which was developed in the late 1960s and early 1970s, began to explain why so many problems in AI were fundamentally hard. Computational complexity cast a long shadow over AI.

We'll begin with the traditional starting point of the golden age: the summer of 1956, when the field was given its name by a young American academic by the name of John McCarthy.

## THE FIRST SUMMER OF AI

McCarthy belonged to that generation who seem to have created the modern technological United States. With almost casual brilliance, throughout the 1950s and 1960s, he invented a range of concepts in computing that are now taken so much for granted that it is hard to imagine that they actually had to be invented. One of his most famous developments was a programming language called LISP, which for decades was the programming language of choice for AI researchers. At the best of times, computer programs are hard to read, but even by the frankly arcane standards of my profession, LISP is regarded as bizarre, because in LISP (all (programs (look (like this))))—generations of programmers learned to joke that LISP stood for Lots of Irrelevant Silly Parentheses.[2]

McCarthy invented LISP in the mid-1950s, but astonishingly, nearly seventy years later, it is still regularly taught and used across the world. (I use it every day.) Think about that for a moment: when McCarthy invented LISP, Dwight D. Eisenhower was president of the United States. There were no more than a handful of computers in the whole world. And the programming language McCarthy invented then is still routinely used today.

In 1955, McCarthy submitted a proposal to the Rockefeller Institute in the hope of obtaining funds to organize a summer school at Dartmouth College. If you are not an academic, the idea of "summer schools" for adults may sound a little strange, but they are a well-established and fondly regarded academic tradition even today. The idea is to bring together a group of researchers with common interests from across the world and give them the opportunity to meet and work together for an extended period. They are held in summer because, of course, teaching has finished for the year, and academics have a big chunk of time without lecturing commitments. Naturally, the goal is to organize the summer school in an attractive location, and a lively program of social events is essential.

When McCarthy wrote his funding proposal for the Rockefeller Institute in 1955, he had to give a name to the event, and he chose *artificial intelligence*. In what would become something of a weary tradition for AI, McCarthy had unrealistically high expectations: "We think that a significant advance can be made ... if a carefully selected group of scientists work on it together for a summer."[3]

By the end of the summer school, the delegates had made no real progress, but McCarthy's chosen name had stuck, and thus was a new academic discipline formed.

Unfortunately, many have subsequently had occasion to regret McCarthy's choice of name for the field he founded. For one thing, *artificial* can be read as *fake* or *ersatz*—and who wants *fake intelligence*? Moreover, the word *intelligence* suggests that *intellect* is key. In fact, many of the tasks that the AI community has worked so hard on since 1956 don't seem to require *intelligence* when people do them. On the contrary, as we saw in the previous chapter, many of the most important and difficult problems that AI has struggled with over the past sixty years don't seem to be *intellectual* at all—a fact that has repeatedly been the cause of consternation and confusion for those new to the field.

But *artificial intelligence* was the name that McCarthy chose and the name that persists to this day. From McCarthy's summer school, there is an unbroken thread of research by way of the participants in the summer school and their academic descendants, right down to the present day. AI in its recognizably modern form began that summer, and the beginnings of AI seemed to be very promising indeed.

The period following the Dartmouth summer school was one of excitement and growth. And for a while at least, it seemed like there was rapid progress. Four delegates of the summer school went on to dominate AI in the decades that followed. McCarthy himself founded the AI lab at Stanford University in the heart of what is now Silicon Valley; Marvin Minsky founded the AI lab at MIT in Cambridge, Massachusetts; and Allen Newell and his Ph.D. supervisor Herb Simon went to Carnegie Mellon University (CMU). These four individuals, and the AI systems that they and their students built, are totems for AI researchers of my generation.

But there was a good deal of naivety in the golden age, with researchers making reckless and grandiose predictions about the likely speed of progress in the field, which have haunted AI ever since. By the mid-1970s, the good times were over, and a vicious backlash began—an AI boom-and-bust cycle destined to be repeated over the coming decades.

## DIVIDE AND CONQUER

As we've seen, general AI is a large and very nebulous target—it is hard to approach directly. Instead, the strategy adopted during the golden age was that of *divide and conquer*. Thus, instead of starting out trying to build a complete general intelligent system, the approach adopted was to identify the various different individual *capabilities* that seemed to be required for general-purpose AI and to build systems that could demonstrate these capabilities. The implicit assumption was that if we could succeed in building systems that demonstrate each of these individual capabilities, then, later on, assembling them into a whole would be straightforward. This fundamental assumption—that the way to progress toward general AI was to focus on the component capabilities of intelligent behavior—became embedded as the standard methodology for AI research. There was a rush to build machines that could demonstrate these component capabilities.

So what were the main capabilities that researchers focused on? The first, and as it turned out one of the most stubbornly difficult, is one that we take for granted: **perception.** A machine that is going to act intelligently in a particular environment needs to be able to get information about it. We perceive our world through various mechanisms, including the five senses: sight, hearing, touch, smell, and taste. So one strand of research involved building **sensors** that provide analogues of these. Robots today use a wide range of artificial sensors to give them information about their environment—radars, infrared range finders, ultrasonic range finders, laser radar, and so on. But *building* these sensors—which in itself is not trivial—is only part of the problem. However good the optics are on a digital camera and no matter how many megapixels there are on the camera's image sensor, ultimately all that camera does is break down the image it is seeing into a grid and then assign numbers to each cell in the grid, indicating color and brightness. So a robot equipped with the very best digital camera will, in the end, only receive a long list of numbers. The second challenge of perception is therefore to interpret those raw numbers: to understand what it is seeing. And this challenge turned out to be far harder than the problem of actually building the sensors.

Another key capability for general intelligent systems seems to be the ability to learn from experience, and this led to a strand of AI research called **machine learning.** Like the name *artificial intelligence* itself, *machine learning* is perhaps an unfortunate choice of terminology. It sounds like a machine somehow bootstrapping its own intelligence: starting from nothing and progressively getting smarter and smarter. In fact, machine learning is not like human learning: it is about learning from and making predictions about data. For example, one big success in machine learning over the past decade is in programs that can recognize faces in pictures. The way this is usually done involves providing a program with examples of the things that you are trying to learn. Thus, a program to recognize faces would be trained by giving it many pictures labeled with the names of the people that appear in the pictures. The goal is that, when subsequently presented with solely an image, the program would be able to correctly give the name of the person pictured.

**Problem solving** and **planning** are two related capabilities that also seem to be associated with intelligent behavior. They both require being able to achieve a goal using a given repertoire of actions; the challenge is to find the right sequence of actions. Playing a board game such as chess or Go would be an example: the goal is to win the game; the actions are the possible moves; the challenge is to figure out which moves to make. As we will see, one of the most fundamental challenges in problem solving and planning is that while they appear easy to do *in principle*, by considering all the possible alternatives, this approach doesn't work in practice, because there are far too many alternatives for it to be feasible.

**Reasoning** is perhaps the most exalted of all the capabilities associated with intelligence: it involves deriving new knowledge from existing facts in a robust way. To pick a famous example, if you know that "all men are mortal" and you know that "Michael is a man," then it is reasonable to conclude that "Michael is mortal." A truly intelligent system would be able to derive this conclusion and then use the newly derived knowledge to make further conclusions. For example, knowing that "Michael is mortal" should then allow you to conclude that "at some point in the future, Michael will die" and that "after Michael is dead, he will stay dead forever," and so on. Automated reasoning is all about giving computers this kind of capability: giving them the capability to reason *logically*. In chapter 3, we will see that for a long time, it was believed that this kind of reasoning should be the main goal for AI, and although this is not a mainstream view anymore, automated reasoning remains an important thread of the field.

Finally, **natural language understanding** involves computers interpreting human languages like English and French. At present, when a programmer gives a computer a recipe to follow (an algorithm or program), she must do so using an *artificial* language: a language specially constructed accordingly to precisely defined unambiguous rules. These languages are *much* simpler than natural languages like English. For a long time, the main approach to understanding natural languages involved trying to come up with precise rules that define these languages, in the same way that we have precise rules defining computer languages. But this turned out to be impossible. Natural languages are too flexible, vague, and fluid to be rigorously defined in this way, and the way in which language is used in everyday situations resists attempts to give it a precise definition.

## SHRDLU AND THE BLOCKS WORLD

The **SHRDLU** system was one of the most acclaimed achievements of the golden age (the odd name derives from the order in which letters were arranged on printing machines of the time—computer programmers enjoy obscure jokes). Developed by Stanford University Ph.D. student Terry Winograd in 1971,[4] SHRDLU aimed to demonstrate two key capabilities for AI: problem solving and natural language understanding.

The problem-solving component of SHRDLU was based around what became one of the most famous experimental scenarios in AI: the **Blocks World.** The Blocks World was a simulated environment containing a number of colored objects (blocks, boxes, and pyramids). The rationale for using a simulated environment, rather than trying to build a real robot, was simply to reduce the complexity of the problem to something manageable. Problem solving in the SHRDLU Blocks World involves arranging objects according to instructions from a user, using a simulated robot arm to manipulate them. Figure 2 illustrates: we see the initial configuration of the Blocks World and the goal configuration. The challenge is to figure out *how* to transform the initial configuration to the goal configuration.

**Figure 2:** The Blocks World. Above is the initial configuration—below, the goal configuration. How do you get from one to the other?

To achieve this transformation, you are only allowed to use a small repertoire of actions:

- ***Pick up object x from the table.*** Here, the robot arm picks up object *x* (which could be a block or pyramid) from the table. The robot arm will only be able to do this successfully if both object *x* is currently on the table and the robot arm is currently empty.

- **Place object x on the table.** The robot arm will only be able to do this if it is currently carrying object *x*.
- **Pick up object x from object y.** For the robot arm to be able to do this, the robot arm must be empty, object *x* must be currently on top of object *y*, and object *x* must currently have nothing on top of it.
- **Place object x on top of object y.** For the robot arm to be able to do this, it has to actually be carrying object *x*, and there must be nothing currently on top of object *y*.

Everything that happens in the Blocks World reduces to these actions, and only these actions. Using these actions, a plan to achieve the transformation illustrated in figure 2 might begin as follows:

- **Pick up object A from object B.**
- **Place object A on the table.**
- **Pick up object B from the table.**

The Blocks World is probably the most-studied scenario in the whole of AI, because tasks in the Blocks World—picking up packages and moving them around—sound like the kind of tasks we might envisage for robots in the real world. But the Blocks World as it appears in SHRDLU (and much subsequent research) has severe limitations as a scenario for developing practically useful AI techniques.

First, it is assumed that the Blocks World is *closed*. This means that the only thing that causes change in the Blocks World is SHRDLU. This is rather like saying that you live alone. If you live alone, you can safely assume that when you wake up, your keys will be where you left them the night before; if you don't live alone, there is always the possibility that someone else has moved them overnight. So when SHRDLU places block *x* on top of block *y*, it can safely assume that block *x* remains on top of block *y* unless it has moved the block itself. The real world is not like that: any AI system that relies on the assumption that it is the only actor in its world is likely to get things wrong a lot of the time.

Second, and perhaps more important, the Blocks World is *simulated*. SHRDLU is not *actually* picking up objects and moving them around with a robot arm—it is just pretending to. It does this by maintaining a model of the world, and it models the effects of its actions on this world. It never actually looks at the world to build its model, or to check that the model it has is correct. This is a huge simplifying assumption, and researchers later argued that it therefore ignored most of the genuinely hard problems that a robot would face in the real world.

To better understand this point, consider the action "Pick up object *x* from object *y*." From the point of view of SHRDLU, this is a single action: the robot is assumed to carry out the *whole* of the action in a single indivisible step, and nowhere does it need to worry about what this action *actually involves*. Thus, all the program "controlling" the arm has to do is to find the right order of such actions to carry out the required task. It doesn't need to worry about the messy business of actually carrying them out. But think about a robot in the physical world trying to undertake this action, perhaps in a warehouse. Here, the robot would have to be able to identify the two objects in question, successfully execute a complex locomotion problem to get the arm to the right place, and grasp the relevant object. Even the final part of this "atomic" action, grasping the relevant object is, in reality, far from trivial—getting robots to manipulate even simple objects in the real world is phenomenally difficult, and remains a significant challenge to the present day. The fact that *we* find such tasks trivial leads us to believe, wrongly, that it must also be trivial to get machines to do them.

So the Blocks World is appealing because it is intuitive and easy to explain, and it seems to resemble a problem that we could imagine robots working on in the real world. But digging deeper, it turns out that it grossly simplifies the problems that would be faced by a real robot.

One of the most lauded features of SHRDLU was that the user gave instructions to the system and received feedback from it in what seemed to be ordinary English. Here is a snippet of dialogue with SHRDLU (SHRDLU's responses are in italics):

> PICK UP A BIG RED BLOCK.
>
> *OK. (Does so.)*
>
> GRASP THE PYRAMID.
>
> *I DON'T UNDERSTAND WHICH PYRAMID YOU MEAN.*
>
> FIND A BLOCK WHICH IS TALLER THAN THE ONE YOU ARE HOLDING AND PUT IT INTO THE BOX.
>
> *BY "IT," I ASSUME YOU MEAN THE BLOCK WHICH IS TALLER THAN THE ONE I AM HOLDING.*
>
> *OK. (Does so.)*
>
> WHAT DOES THE BOX CONTAIN?
>
> *THE BLUE PYRAMID AND THE BLUE BLOCK.*
>
> WHAT IS THE PYRAMID SUPPORTED BY?
>
> *THE BOX.*
>
> HOW MANY BLOCKS ARE NOT IN THE BOX?
>
> *FOUR OF THEM.*
>
> IS AT LEAST ONE OF THEM NARROWER THAN THE ONE WHICH I TOLD YOU TO PICK UP?
>
> *YES, THE RED CUBE.*

This dialogue is far beyond ELIZA,[5] and it was this aspect of the system—the way that a user interacted with it, via what seemed at first like ordinary English—which led to SHRDLU receiving a rapturous reception in the early 1970s. However, it later became clear that SHRDLU was able to generate rich dialogues only because those dialogues related to a very constrained scenario—the Blocks World. The dialogues were not quite "canned" in the way that dialogues in ELIZA were canned, but they were, nevertheless, very constrained. There was hope, when the system first appeared, that the techniques it embodied might provide a route to much more general natural-language understanding systems, but this hope was not realized.

It is easy for us, fifty years later, to identify the limitations of SHRDLU. But it was hugely influential, and remains one of the landmark AI systems.

## SHAKEY THE ROBOT

Robots have always been closely associated with AI—particularly in the media. The "machine man" in Fritz Lang's classic 1927 film *Metropolis* set the template for the endless portrayals of robotic AI that followed: a robot with two arms, two legs, a head . . . and a murderous temperament. Even today, it seems, every article about AI in the popular press is illustrated with a picture of a robot that could be a direct descendant of the *Metropolis* "machine man." It is, I think, no surprise that robots in general, and humanoid robots in particular, should become the public signifier for AI. After all, the idea of robots that inhabit our world and work among us is probably the most obvious manifestation of the AI dream—and most of us would be delighted to have robot butlers to do our every bidding.

It may therefore come as a surprise to learn that during the golden age, robots were only a comparatively small part of the AI story. I'm afraid the reasons for this are rather mundane: building robots is expensive, time-consuming, and, frankly, *difficult*. It would have been impossible for a Ph.D. student working alone in the 1960s or 1970s to build a research-level AI robot. They would have needed an entire research lab, dedicated engineers, and workshop facilities—and in any case, computers powerful enough to drive AI programs were not mobile enough to install on autonomous robots. It was easier and much cheaper for researchers to build programs like SHRDLU, which *pretended* to be working in the real world, than it was to build robots that *actually* operated in the real world, with all its complexity and messiness.

But although the roster of AI robots in the early period of AI is rather sparse, there was one glorious experiment with AI robots during this time: the **SHAKEY** project, which was carried out at the Stanford Research Institute (SRI) between 1966 and 1972.

SHAKEY was the first serious attempt to build a mobile robot that could be given tasks in the real world and that could figure out on its own how to accomplish them. To do this, SHAKEY had to be able to perceive its environment and understand where it was and what was around it; receive tasks from users; figure out for itself appropriate plans to achieve those tasks; and then actually carry out these plans, all the while making sure that everything was progressing as intended. The tasks in question involved moving objects such as boxes around an office environment. This may sound like SHRDLU, but unlike SHRDLU, SHAKEY was a real robot, manipulating real objects. This was a far greater challenge.

To succeed, SHAKEY had to integrate a daunting array of AI capabilities. First, there was a basic engineering challenge: the developers needed to build the robot itself. It had to be small enough and agile enough to operate in an office, and it needed sensors that were powerful and accurate enough that the robot could understand what was around it. For this, SHAKEY was equipped with a television camera and laser range finders for determining distance to objects; to detect obstacles, it had bump detectors, called *cats' whiskers*. Next, SHAKEY had to be able to navigate around its environment. Then, SHAKEY needed to be able to plan how to carry out the tasks it was given.[6] And finally, all these capabilities had to be made to work together in harmony. As any AI researcher will tell you, getting any one of these components to work is a challenge in itself; getting them to work as an ensemble is an order of magnitude harder.

But impressive as it was, SHAKEY also highlighted the limitations of the AI technology of the time. To make SHAKEY work, its designers had to greatly simplify the challenges faced by the robot. For example, SHAKEY's ability to interpret data from its TV camera was very limited—amounting to not much more than detecting obstacles. And even to enable this, the environment had to be specially painted and carefully lit. Because the TV camera required so much power, it was only switched on when it was needed, and it took about ten seconds after the power was turned on before it produced a usable image. And the developers constantly struggled with the limitations of computers at that time: it took up to fifteen minutes for SHAKEY to figure out how to carry out a task, during which time SHAKEY would sit, immobile and inert, utterly isolated from its environment. Since computers with sufficient power to run SHAKEY's software were too large and heavy for SHAKEY to carry around, SHAKEY used a radio link to a computer that actually ran its software.[7] Overall, SHAKEY could not possibly have been put to use on any substantial problem.

SHAKEY was arguably the first real autonomous mobile robot, and like SHRDLU, it deserves a place of honor in the AI history books for this reason. But SHAKEY's limitations demonstrated just how far AI actually was from the dream of practical autonomous robots and just how daunting these challenges really were.

## PROBLEM SOLVING AND SEARCH

The ability to solve complex problems is surely one of the key capabilities that distinguishes humans from other animals. And of course, problem solving seems like the kind of thing that requires intelligence—if we can build programs that can solve problems that people find hard, then surely this would be a key step on the road to AI. Problem solving was therefore studied intensely during the golden age, and a standard exercise for AI researchers of the time was to get a computer to solve a problem of the kind that you might come across on the puzzle page of a newspaper. Here is a classic example of such a puzzle, called the Towers of Hanoi:

In a remote monastery, there are three columns and sixty-four golden rings. The rings are of different sizes and rest over the columns. Initially, all the rings rested on the farthest left column, and since then, the monks have been moving the rings, one by one, between columns. Their goal is to move all the rings to the farthest right column. In doing so, the monks must obey two rules:

1. They may only move one ring at a time between columns.

2. At no time may any ring rest upon a smaller ring.

So to solve the problem, you have to find the right sequence of moves, which will get all the rings from the farthest left column to the farthest right one, without breaking the rule that a larger ring can never be above a smaller ring.

In some versions of the story, the world is supposed to end when the monks complete their task—although, as we will see later, even if this story were true, we would not need to lose sleep over it, because life on planet Earth will surely be extinct long before the monks would be able to move all sixty-four rings. For this reason, the puzzle is usually deployed with far fewer rings. Figure 3 illustrates the puzzle, showing the initial configuration (all rings are on the farthest left column), then the goal state (with all rings on the farthest right column), and finally an illegal configuration, for the three-ring version of the puzzle.

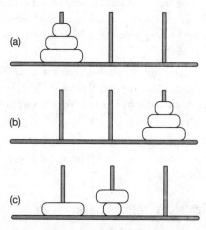

**Figure 3:** The Towers of Hanoi, a classic puzzle of the type studied in the golden age of AI. Panel (a) shows the initial state of the puzzle, and panel (b) shows the goal state. Panel (c) shows a disallowed configuration of the puzzle (it isn't allowed because a larger ring is on top of a smaller ring).

So how do we go about solving problems like the Towers of Hanoi? The answer is to use a technique called **search.** I should clarify that when we use the term *search* in AI, we don't mean searching the web: search in AI is a problem-solving technique, which involves systematically considering all possible courses of action. Any program that plays a game like chess will be based on search, as will the satellite navigation system in your car. Search arises time and time again: it is one of the cornerstone techniques in AI.

All problems like the Towers of Hanoi have the same basic structure. As in the Blocks World, we want to find a sequence of actions that will take us from some **initial state** of the problem to some designated **goal state.** The term **state** is used in

AI to refer to a particular configuration of a problem at some moment in time.

We can use search to solve problems like the Towers of Hanoi through the following procedure:

- First, starting from the initial state, we consider the effects of every available action on that initial state. The effect of performing an action is to transform the problem into a new state.

- If one of the actions has generated the goal state, then we have succeeded: the solution to the puzzle is the sequence of actions that got us from the initial state to the goal state.

- Otherwise, we repeat this process for every state we just generated, considering the effect of each action on those states, and so on.

Applying this recipe for search generates a **search tree:**

- Initially, we can only move the smallest ring, and our only choices are to move it to the middle or farthest right column. So we have two possible actions available for the first move and two possible successor states.

- If we chose to move the small ring to the center column (shown via the left arrow emerging from the initial state), then we subsequently have three possible actions available to us: we can move the smallest ring to the farthest left column or the farthest right column, or we can move the middle-sized ring to the farthest right column (we can't move it to the center column, because then it would be on top of the smallest ring, which violates the rules of the puzzle).

- . . . and so on.

Because we are systematically generating the search tree, level by level, we are considering all possibilities—and so if there is a solution, we will be guaranteed to eventually find it using this process.

So how many moves would you need to make to solve the Towers of Hanoi problem *optimally* (i.e., with the smallest possible number of moves from the initial state)? The answer, for three rings, turns out to be seven: you will never be able to find a solution that solves the puzzle in fewer than seven moves. There are solutions that solve it in more than seven moves (in fact there are *infinitely many* such solutions) but they are not optimal, because you could have done it in fewer. Now, because the search process we have described is exhaustive—in the sense that it will systematically unwind the search tree, considering all possibilities at every stage—it is guaranteed not just to find a solution but to find the *shortest* solution.

**Figure 4:** A small fragment of the search tree for the Towers of Hanoi puzzle.

So this process of naive exhaustive search is guaranteed to find a solution to the problem if one exists, and it is also guaranteed to find the shortest solution. Moreover, as computational recipes go, exhaustive search is pretty simple—it is easy to write a program to implement this recipe.

But even a cursory study of the search tree in figure 4 shows that, in the simple form we just described it, naive exhaustive search is actually a pretty stupid process. For example, if you study the leftmost branch of the search tree, you will see that, after just two moves, we have returned to the initial state of the problem, which seems like a pointless waste of effort. If *you* were solving the Towers of Hanoi, you might make this mistake once or twice while looking for a solution, but you would quickly learn to spot and avoid such wasted effort. But a computer carrying out the recipe for naive exhaustive search does not: the recipe involves systematically generating all the alternatives, even if those alternatives are a waste of time, in the sense that they are revisiting earlier failed configurations.

But apart from being hopelessly inefficient, exhaustive search has a much more fundamental problem. If you do a little experimentation, you will see that in almost all possible configurations of the Towers of Hanoi puzzle, you will have three possible moves available to you. We say that the **branching factor** of the puzzle is three. Different search problems will have different branching factors. In the board game Go, for example, the branching factor is 250, meaning that, on average, each player will have about 250 moves available in any given state of the game. So let's look at how the *size* of a search tree grows with respect to the branching factor of the tree—how many states there will be in any given level of the tree. So consider the game of Go:[8]

- The first level of the tree will contain 250 states, because there are 250 moves available from the initial state of the game.
- The second level of the search tree will have 250 × 250 = 62,500 states, because we have to consider each possible move for each of the 250 states in the first level of the tree.
- The third level of the search tree will contain 250 × 62,500 = 15.6 million states.
- The fourth level of the search tree will contain 250 × 15.6 million = 3.9 billion states.

So at the time of writing, a typical desktop computer would not have enough memory to be able to store the search tree for the game of Go for more than about four moves—and a typical game of Go lasts for about 200 moves. The number of states in the Go search tree for 200 moves is a number that is so large that it defies comprehension. It is hundreds of orders of magnitude larger than the number of atoms in our universe. No improvement in conventional computer technology is ever going to be able to cope with search trees this large.

Search trees grow fast. Ludicrously, unimaginably fast. This problem is called **combinatorial explosion,** and it is the single most important practical problem in AI, because search is such a ubiquitous requirement in AI problems.[9] If you could find a foolproof recipe for solving search problems quickly—to get the same result as exhaustive search, without all that effort—then you would make yourself very famous, and many problems that are currently very difficult for AI would suddenly become easy. But you won't, I'm afraid. We can't get around combinatorial explosion: we need to work with it. Attention therefore shifted to making search more efficient. To do this, there are several obvious lines of attack.

One possibility is to *focus* the search in some way—to identify promising directions in the search tree and explore those, rather than trying to explore them all. A simple way of doing this is as follows: instead of developing the tree level by level, we instead build the tree *along just one branch.* This approach is called **depth-first search.** With depth-first search, we carry on expanding a branch until we get a solution or become convinced that we won't get a solution; if we ever get stuck (for example by re-creating a configuration that we already saw, as in the farthest left branch of figure 4), then we stop expanding that branch and go back up the tree to start working on the next branch.

The main advantage that depth-first search has is that we don't have to store the whole of the search tree: we only need to store the branch we are working on. But it has a big disadvantage: if we pick the wrong branch to explore, then we may go on expanding our search along this branch without ever finding a solution. So if we want to use depth-first search, we really want to know which branch to investigate. And this is what **heuristic search** tries to help us with.

The idea of heuristic search is to use rules of thumb called **heuristics,** which indicate where to focus our search. We can't typically find heuristics that are *guaranteed* to focus search in the best possible direction, but we can often find heuristics that work well in cases of interest.

Heuristic search is such a natural idea that it has been reinvented many times over the years, and so it seems pointless to debate who invented it. But we can identify with reasonable confidence the first substantial application of heuristic search in an AI program: a program to play the game of checkers, written by an IBM employee called Arthur Samuel in the mid-1950s. Perhaps the key component of Samuel's program was a way of evaluating any given board position, to estimate how "good" the position was for a particular player: intuitively, a "good" board position for a particular player is one that would probably lead to a win for that player, whereas a "bad" board position would probably lead to that player losing. To do this, Samuel used a number of *features* of the board position in order to compute its value. For example, one feature might be the number of pieces you have on the board: the more you have, the better you are doing. These different features were then aggregated by the program to give a single overall measure of the quality of a board position. Then a typical heuristic would involve picking a move that leads to the best board position, according to this heuristic.

Samuel's program played a credible game of checkers. This

was an impressive achievement in many respects but is all the more so when one considers the primitive state of practical computers of the time—the IBM 701 computer that Samuel used could only handle programs that were the equivalent length of just a few pages of text. A modern desktop computer will have millions of times more memory than this and will be millions of times faster. Given these restrictions, it is impressive that it could play the game at all, let alone play it competently.

## AI CRASHES INTO THE COMPLEXITY BARRIER

We previously saw that computers were for all intents and purposes invented by Alan Turing in order to solve one of the great mathematical problems of his time. It is one of the great ironies of scientific history that Turing invented computers in order to show that there are things that computers are fundamentally incapable of doing—that some problems are inherently undecidable.

In the decades following Turing's results, exploring the limits of what computers can and cannot do became a small industry in university mathematics departments across the world. The focus in this work was on separating out those problems that are inherently undecidable (cannot be solved by computer) from those that are decidable (can be solved by computer). One intriguing discovery from this time was that there are *hierarchies* of undecidable problems: it is possible to have a problem that is not just undecidable but *highly* undecidable. (This kind of thing is catnip for mathematicians of a certain type.)

But by the 1960s, it was becoming clear that whether a problem is or is not decidable was far from being the end of the story. The fact that a problem was decidable in the sense of Turing's work did not mean that it was *practically* solvable at all: some problems that were solvable according to Turing's theory seemed to resist all practical attempts to attack them—they required impossible amounts of memory or were too impossibly slow to ever be practicable. And it was becoming uncomfortably obvious that many AI problems fell into this awkward class.

Here's an example of a problem that is easily seen to be solvable according to Turing's theory—the problem is rather famous, as computational problems go, and you may have heard of it. It is called the *traveling salesman problem*.[10]

A salesman must visit a group of cities in a road network, returning finally to his starting point. Not all the cities are connected by road, but for those that are, the salesman knows the shortest route. The salesman's car can drive for a certain, known number of miles on a single tank of gas. Is there a route for the salesman, which will visit all the cities and return to the starting destination, which can be done on a single tank of gas?

We can solve this problem, using naive search, just by listing all the possible tours of the cities and checking whether each tour is possible on a single tank of gas. However, as you might now guess, the number of possible tours increases very rapidly as the number of cities increases: for 10 cities, you would have to consider up to 3.6 million possible tours; for 11 cities, you would have to consider up to 40 million.

This is another example of combinatorial explosion. We were introduced to combinatorial explosion when looking at search trees, where each successive layer in the search tree multiplies the size of the tree. Combinatorial explosion occurs in situations where you must make a series of successive choices: each successive choice *multiplies* the total number of possible outcomes.

So our naive approach, of exhaustively searching through all the candidate tours, is not going to be feasible. It works *in principle* (given enough time, we will get the right answer), but it doesn't work *in practice* (because the amount of time required to consider all the alternatives quickly becomes impossibly large).

But as we noted earlier, naive exhaustive search is a very crude technique. We could use heuristics, but they aren't guaranteed to work. Is there a *smarter* way that is *guaranteed* to find an appropriate tour, which doesn't involve exhaustively checking all the alternatives? *No!* You might find a technique that improves things marginally, but ultimately, *you won't be able to get around that combinatorial explosion.* Any recipe you find that is guaranteed to solve this problem is not going to be feasible for most cases of interest.

The reason for this is that our problem is an example of what is called an **NP-complete** problem. I'm afraid the acronym is not helpful for the uninitiated: *NP* stands for *non-deterministic polynomial time,* and the technical meaning is rather complex. Fortunately, the intuition behind NP-complete problems is simple.

An NP-complete problem is a combinatorial problem, like the traveling salesman problem, in which it is *hard to find solutions* (because there are too many of them to exhaustively consider each one, as we discussed above) but where it is *easy to verify whether you have found a solution* (in the traveling salesman problem, we can check a possible solution by simply verifying that the tour is possible on a single tank of gas).

To date, nobody has found an efficient recipe for any NP-complete problem. And the question of whether NP-complete problems can be efficiently solved is, in fact, one of the most important open problems in science today. It is called the **P-versus-NP problem,**[11] and if you can settle it one way or the other to the satisfaction of the scientific community, you stand to receive a prize of $1 million from the Clay Mathematics Institute, who in the year 2000 identified it as one of the "millennium problems" in mathematics. Smart money says that NP-complete problems *cannot* be solved efficiently; but smart money also says that we are a long way from knowing for certain whether this really is the case.

If you discover that a problem you are working on is NP-complete, then this tells you that techniques to solve it based on simple brute force are just not going to work: your problem is, in a precise mathematical sense, *hard.*

The basic structure of NP-complete problems was unraveled in the early 1970s, and researchers in AI started to look at the problems that they had been working on using the new theory. The results were shocking. Everywhere they looked—in problem solving, game playing, planning, learning, reasoning—it seemed that key problems were NP-complete (or worse). The phenomenon was so ubiquitous that it became a joke—the term *AI-complete* came to mean "a problem as hard as AI itself"—if you could solve one AI-complete problem, so the joke went, you would solve them all.

Before the theory of NP-completeness and its consequences were understood, there was always a hope that some sudden breakthrough would render these problems easy—**tractable,** to use the technical term. And technically, such a hope still remains, since we don't yet know for certain that NP-complete problems cannot be solved efficiently. But by the late 1970s, the specter of NP-completeness and combinatorial explosion began to loom large over the AI landscape. The field had hit a barrier, in the form of computational complexity, and progress ground to a halt. The techniques developed in the golden age seemed unable to scale up beyond toy scenarios like the Blocks World, and the optimistic predictions of rapid progress made throughout the 1950s and 1960s started to haunt the early pioneers.

## AI AS ALCHEMY

By the early 1970s, the wider scientific community was beginning to be more and more frustrated by the very visible lack of progress made on core AI problems and by the continuing extravagant claims of some researchers. By the mid-1970s, the criticisms reached a fever pitch.

Of all the critics (and there were many), the most outspoken was the American philosopher Hubert Dreyfus. He was commissioned by the RAND Corporation in the mid-1960s to write a report on the state of progress in AI. The title he chose for his report, *Alchemy and AI*, made very clear his disdain for the field and those who worked in it. Publicly equating the work of a serious scientist to alchemy is extraordinarily insulting. Rereading *Alchemy and AI* now, the contempt is palpable and still rather shocking more than half a century later.

While we might frown upon the way in which Dreyfus articulated his critique of AI, it is hard to avoid the conclusion that he had a few valid points—particularly about the inflated claims and grand predictions of AI pioneers. In hindsight, it is painfully obvious that such claims and predictions were hopelessly unrealistic. I think at least some of this exuberance should be forgiven. In particular, there was no reason to suppose that the problems being tackled were *by their very nature* hard for computers to solve. Back then, there had always been the possibility that some breakthrough would render the difficult problems easy. But when understanding of NP-completeness began to spread, the community began to understand what it really meant for a computational problem to be *hard*.

## THE END OF THE GOLDEN AGE

In 1972, a key funding body for scientific research in the UK asked the eminent mathematician Sir James Lighthill to evaluate the state of and prospects for AI. The request supposedly came after reports of academic infighting among members of the AI community at the University of Edinburgh, then and now one of the world's leading centers for AI research. Lighthill was at the time Lucasian Professor of Mathematics at the

University of Cambridge, the most prestigious academic position that can be held by a UK mathematician (his successor in the post was Stephen Hawking). He had a wealth of experience in practical applied mathematics. However, reading the *Lighthill Report* today, he seems to have been left utterly bemused by his exposure to the AI culture of the time. His report was fiercely dismissive of mainstream AI—he specifically identified combinatorial explosion as a key problem that the AI community had failed to tackle. His report immediately led to severe funding cuts to AI research across the UK.

In the United States, the main funders of AI research historically had been the military funding agency DARPA and its predecessor, ARPA, but by the early 1970s, they too were becoming frustrated with the failure of AI to deliver on its many promises. Funding cuts to AI research in the United States followed.

The decade from the early 1970s to the early 1980s later became known as the **AI winter,** although it should perhaps better be known as the *first* AI winter, because there were more to come. The stereotype was established, of AI researchers making hopelessly overoptimistic and unwarranted predictions, then failing to deliver. Within the scientific community, AI began to acquire a reputation somewhat akin to homeopathic medicine. As a serious academic discipline, it appeared to be in terminal decline.

# 3

# Knowledge Is Power

IT IS IMPORTANT not to underestimate the damage inflicted on AI during the mid-1970s. Many academics started to treat AI as a pseudoscience—the field has really only recently recovered from the reputational damage it suffered during the AI winter. But even as the *Lighthill Report* was being circulated and its consequences were being felt, a new approach to AI was beginning to gain attention, which promised to overcome the problems that had led to AI getting such bad press. The problem with previous efforts, according to a new generation of researchers that burst onto the scene in the late 1970s and early 1980s was that AI had focused too much on general approaches like search and problem solving. These "weak" methods, it was argued, were missing a key ingredient that must surely be a crucial part of any intelligent activity: *knowledge.* The proponents of knowledge-based AI were convinced that capturing and using human knowledge was the key to progress in AI.

A new class of knowledge-based AI systems began to emerge. These so-called **expert systems** used human expert knowledge to solve specific, narrowly defined problems. Expert systems provided evidence that AI systems could outperform humans in certain tasks, and perhaps more important, for the first time, they showed that AI could be applied to problems of commercial interest—AI suddenly showed the potential to make money. And it was possible to teach the techniques of knowledge-based AI to a wide audience—a generation of graduates emerged determined to apply their practical AI skills.

Expert systems made no claim to be general AI. Rather, the aim was to build systems that could solve very narrow, very specific problems that required considerable human expertise. Typically, these were problems in which a human expert had acquired expertise over a long period of time and where that human expertise was scarce.

For the next decade, knowledge-based expert systems were the main focus of AI research. Enormous investment from industry flowed into the field. By the early 1980s, the AI winter was over—another, much bigger AI boom was under way.

In this chapter, we'll look at the expert systems boom, which lasted from the late 1970s to the late 1980s. We'll start by seeing how human expert knowledge can be captured and given to computers, and I'll tell you the story of MYCIN—one of the most celebrated expert systems of the period. We'll see how researchers looked to try to build richer ways of capturing knowledge, using the power and precision of mathematical logic—and how this goal ultimately foundered. We'll then hear the story of one of the most ambitious and notorious failed projects in AI history—the Cyc project, which tried to use human expert knowledge to solve the biggest problem of them all: general AI.

## CAPTURING HUMAN KNOWLEDGE USING RULES

The idea of using knowledge in AI systems was arguably not a new one. Heuristics, as we saw in the previous chapter, were widely used in the golden age as a means to focus problem solving in promising directions. Such heuristics can be understood as embodying knowledge about a problem. But heuristics only capture knowledge *implicitly*. Knowledge-based AI was based on an important new idea: that human knowledge about a problem should be *explicitly* captured and *represented* within an AI system.

The most common scheme adopted for what came to be called **knowledge representation** was based on **rules.** A rule in the context of AI captures a discrete chunk of knowledge, in the form of an if-then expression. Rules are actually rather simple and best explained by way of an example, so following are some rules (written in English), which are part of the folklore of AI.[1] They capture knowledge for an expert system that assists a user in the task of classifying animals:

> **IF animal gives milk THEN animal is mammal**
>
> **IF animal has feathers THEN animal is bird**
>
> **IF animal can fly AND animal lays eggs THEN animal is bird**
>
> **IF animal eats meat THEN animal is carnivore**

The way we interpret such rules is as follows: each rule has an **antecedent** (the part after the IF) and a **consequent** (the part after the THEN). For example, in the following rule:

> **IF animal can fly AND animal lays eggs THEN animal is bird**

the antecedent is "animal can fly AND animal lays eggs," while the consequent is "animal is bird." The usual interpretation of such a rule is that if the information that we currently have correctly matches the antecedent, then the rule **fires,** meaning that we may then conclude the consequent. For this rule to fire, we would therefore require two pieces of information: that the animal we are trying to classify can fly, and the animal we are trying to classify lays eggs. If we do indeed have this information, then the rule fires, and we conclude that the animal is a bird. This conclusion gives us more information, which can then be used in subsequent rules to obtain more information, and so on. Usually, expert systems interacted with a user, in the form of a consultation. The user would be responsible for providing information to the system, and answering questions posed by the system.

## MYCIN: A CLASSIC EXPERT SYSTEM

Of the first generation of expert systems that emerged in the 1970s, perhaps the most iconic was **MYCIN**[2] (the name derives from the fact that many antibiotics have *-mycin* as a suffix). MYCIN demonstrated, for the first time, that AI systems could outperform human experts in important problems and provided the template for countless systems that followed.

MYCIN was intended to be a doctor's assistant, providing expert advice about blood diseases in humans. The system was developed by a team of researchers at Stanford University, including experts from Stanford's AI labs, led by Bruce Buchanan, and experts from Stanford's medical school, led by Ted Shortliffe. The fact that the project benefited directly from the commitment of the people who actually knew the stuff the expert system was supposed to be expert in was a key factor in the success of MYCIN. Many later expert system projects failed because they lacked the necessary buy-in from the relevant human experts.

MYCIN's knowledge about blood diseases was represented using a slightly richer form of rules than we used in the animals example above. A typical MYCIN rule (expressed in English) is as follows:

**IF:**

**1) The organism does not stain using the Gram method**

**AND**

**2) The morphology of the organism is rod**

**AND**

**3) The organism is anaerobic**

**THEN**

**There is evidence (0.6) that the organism is bacteroides.**

MYCIN's knowledge about blood disease was encoded and refined over a period of about five years. In its final version, the knowledge base contained hundreds of rules like this. MYCIN became iconic because it embodied all the key features that came to be regarded as essential for expert systems.

First, the operation of the system was intended to resemble a consultation with a human user—a sequence of questions to the user, to which the user provides responses. This became the standard model for expert systems, and MYCIN's main role—diagnosis—became a standard task for expert systems.

Second, MYCIN was able to *explain* its reasoning. This issue—the transparency of reasoning—became crucially important for applications of AI. If an AI system is operating on a problem that has significant consequences (in the case of MYCIN, potentially life-or-death consequences), then it is essential that those who are asked to follow the system's recommendations have confidence in them, and for this, the ability to explain and justify a recommendation is essential. Experience shows that systems operating as black boxes, making recommendations without the ability to justify them, are treated with great suspicion by users.

Crucially, MYCIN was able to answer questions relating to why it had reached a particular conclusion. It did this by producing the chain of reasoning that led to the conclusion—the rules that were fired and the information that had been obtained leading to these rules being fired. In practice, the explanation capabilities of most expert systems ultimately boiled down to something similar. While not ideal, such explanations are easy to produce and give at least some mechanism through which to understand the system's conclusions.

Finally, MYCIN was able to cope with **uncertainty:** situations in which the information provided was not known to be true with certainty. Handling uncertainty turned out to be a ubiquitous requirement for expert system applications and AI systems more generally. In systems like MYCIN, it is rarely the case that a definite conclusion can be drawn on the basis of a particular piece of evidence. For example, when a user has a blood test that comes back positive, then that provides some useful evidence that can be taken into consideration by the system, but there will always be the possibility of a faulty test (a false positive or false negative). Alternatively, if a patient displays some symptom, then this may be *indicative* of a particular ailment, but not enough to conclude with certainty that the patient suffers from the ailment. To be able to make good judgments, expert systems need to be able to take such evidence into account in a principled way.

In trials carried out in 1979, MYCIN's performance in diagnosing blood diseases was shown to be at a comparable level to human experts when evaluated on ten real cases, and above the level of general practitioners. This was one of the first times that an AI system demonstrated capabilities at or above human expert level in a task of real significance.

## BOOM TIMES AGAIN

MYCIN was just one of a number of high-profile expert systems that appeared in the 1970s. The **DENDRAL** project, also from Stanford University, was led by Ed Feigenbaum, who became one of the best-known advocates of knowledge-based systems and is often regarded as the "father of expert systems." DENDRAL aimed to help chemists determine the chemical structure of a compound from the information provided by mass spectrometers. By the mid-1980s, DENDRAL was being used by hundreds of people every day.

The **R1/XCON** system was developed by Digital Equipment Corporation (DEC) in order to help configure their popular VAX computers. By the end of the 1980s, the system had about 17,500 rules, and the developers claimed it had saved the company about $40 million.

DENDRAL showed that expert systems could be useful, MYCIN showed they could outperform human experts at their own game, and R1/XCON showed that they could make serious money.

These success stories attracted a lot of interest: AI, it seemed, was ready for business. Massive investment flowed in. A flurry of start-up companies rushed to cash in on the boom. Companies across the world scrambled to get in on the expert systems boom—and not just software companies. By the 1980s, industry was beginning to understand that knowledge and expertise were important assets that could be nurtured and developed, to profitable advantage. Expert systems seemed to make this intangible asset tangible. The concept of a knowledge-based system resonated with the then prevailing view that Western economies were entering a postindustrial period, in which new opportunities for economic development would come primarily from the so-called knowledge-based industries and services rather than from manufacturing and other traditional industries. A grand new job title emerged: **knowledge engineer.**

## LOGICAL AI

Although rules became established as the de facto knowledge representation scheme for expert systems, the issue of knowledge representation troubled AI researchers. One problem was that rules were just too simple to capture knowledge about complex environments. Rules of the type used in MYCIN were not well suited to capturing knowledge about environments that change over time, or that contain multiple actors (human or AI), or where there is uncertainty about the actual state of the environment. Another problem was that researchers wanted to understand what the knowledge in their expert systems actually *meant*, and to be sure that the reasoning that the system undertook was robust. In short, they wanted to provide a proper mathematical basis for knowledge-based systems.

The solution that began to emerge in the late 1970s was to use **logic** as a unifying scheme for knowledge representation. To understand the role that logic played in knowledge-based systems, it helps to know a little about what logic is and why it was developed. Logic was developed in order to understand reasoning, and in particular, what distinguishes good (**sound**) **reasoning** from bad (**unsound**) **reasoning.** Let's see some examples of reasoning, both sound and unsound.

> *All humans are mortal.*
>
> *Emma is human.*
>
> *Therefore, Emma is mortal.*

This example illustrates a particular pattern of logical reasoning called a **syllogism.** And I hope you will agree that the reasoning here is perfectly reasonable: if all humans are mortal, and Emma is human, then Emma is indeed mortal.

Now consider the following example:

> *All professors are good-looking.*
>
> *Michael is a professor.*
>
> *Therefore, Michael is good-looking.*

You may be less comfortable with this example, because while you were happy to accept the statement "All humans are mortal," you would probably balk at the statement "All professors are good-looking"—it obviously isn't true. However, from a *logical* point of view, there is nothing at all wrong with the reasoning in this example: it is perfectly sound. If it were indeed the case that all professors are good-looking, and it was also the case that Michael is a professor, then it would be entirely reasonable to conclude that Michael is good-looking. Logic is not concerned with whether the statements you start from (the **premises**) are *actually* true or not, simply whether the pattern of reasoning you use and the conclusions you draw would be reasonable if the premises were indeed true.

The next example, however, shows some unsound reasoning:

> **All students are hardworking.**
>
> **Sophie is a student.**
>
> **Therefore, Sophie is rich.**

The pattern of reasoning here is not sound, because it is not reasonable to draw the conclusion that Sophie is rich given the two premises. Sophie *may* be rich, but that isn't the point, which is that you can't reasonably derive this conclusion from the two given premises.

So logic is all about patterns of reasoning, of which syllogisms as shown in the first two examples above are perhaps the simplest useful examples. Logic tells us when we can safely draw conclusions from premises, and the process through which this is done is called **deduction.**

Syllogisms were introduced by the ancient Greek philosopher Aristotle, and for more than a millennium, they provided the main framework for logical analysis. However, they capture a very limited form of logical reasoning, completely inappropriate for many forms of argument. From early on, mathematicians have had a strong interest in trying to understand the general principles of sound reasoning, as mathematics is, ultimately, all about reasoning: the job of a mathematician is to derive new mathematical knowledge from existing knowledge—making deductions, in other words. By the nineteenth century, mathematicians were troubled about the principles of what they were doing. What does it mean, they wondered, for something to be true? How can we be sure that a mathematical proof represents a reasonable deduction? How can we even be sure that $1 + 1 = 2$?

From about the mid-nineteenth century, mathematicians started to investigate these questions in earnest. In Germany, Gottlob Frege developed a general logical calculus within which we can for the first time start to see something resembling the full framework of modern mathematical logic. Augustus De Morgan in London, and George Boole in Cork, Ireland, started to show how the same kinds of techniques that are used for problems of algebra can be applied to logical reasoning. (In 1854, Boole published some of his findings under the gloriously immodest title of *The Laws of Thought.*)

By the start of the twentieth century, the basic framework of modern logic had been largely established, and a logical system had emerged that to the present day provides the language that underpins almost all work in mathematics. The system goes by the name of **first-order logic**. First-order logic is the lingua franca of mathematics and reasoning. Within this one framework, we can capture all the types of reasoning studied by Aristotle, Frege, De Morgan, Boole, and others. And in just the same way, within AI, first-order logic seemed to offer a rich, general framework for capturing human knowledge.

The paradigm of **logic-based AI** was thus born, and one of its earliest and most influential advocates was John McCarthy. McCarthy described his vision for logical AI as follows:[3]

> The idea is that an agent can represent knowledge of its world, its goals and the current situation by sentences in logic and decide what to do by [deducing] that a certain action or course of action is appropriate to achieve its goals.

The "agent" here is the AI system; the "sentences in logic" that McCarthy refers to are precisely the statements like "All humans are mortal" and "All professors are good-looking" that we saw above. First-order logic provides a rich, mathematically precise language with which such statements may be expressed.

**Figure 5:** McCarthy's vision for logic-based AI. A logic-based AI system explicitly represents its beliefs about the environment via logical statements, and intelligent decision-making is broken down into a process of logical reasoning.

A (rather stylized) illustration of McCarthy's vision for logical AI is shown in figure 5. We see a robot operating in a Blocks World type of environment. The robot is equipped with a robot arm and with a perception system that is used to obtain information about its environment. Within the robot, we see a logical description of the environment, with statements like "On(A, Table)," "On(C, A)," and so on. These statements are in fact expressions of first-order logic, and for the scenario shown in figure 5, it is pretty obvious what they are intended to mean:

- **On(x, y)** means that the object *x* is on top of object *y*;
- **Clear(x)** means that there is nothing on top of object *x*; and
- **Empty(x)** means that *x* is empty.

The role of the internal logical representation for the robot is to capture all the information that the agent has about its environment. It became common to refer to this representation as the **beliefs** of the system. The fact that the robot's belief system contains the expression "On(A, Table)" is then taken to mean that "the robot believes that block A is on the table." We need to be careful with such terminology, though. While it is helpful to use a vocabulary that we are familiar with when we populate the robot's belief system ("On(*x, y*)" is pretty self-explanatory for human readers), the *meaning* of an expression such as this, when present in the robot's belief base, is ultimately derived from the *role it plays in the behavior of the robot*. It only really counts as a belief if, when the robot has this in its knowledge base, the robot acts as if it believes that *x* is on top of *y*.

The task of the perception system in figure 5 is to translate the raw information provided by the robot's sensors into the internal logical form used by the robot. As we have already mentioned, this is by no means a trivial thing to do, a point to which we will return later.

Finally, the actual behavior of the robot is defined through the robot's logical deduction system (its **inference engine**). The core idea in logical AI is that the robot reasons logically about what it should do: it *deduces* what it should do next.

Overall, we can envisage the robot continually operating on a cycle of observing its environment through its sensors, updating its beliefs about its environment, deducing what the next action to perform should be, performing this action, and then starting the whole process again.

It is important to understand why logic-based AI was so influential. Perhaps the most important reason is that it makes everything so *pure*. The whole problem of building an intelligent system is reduced to one of constructing a logical description of what the robot should do. And such a system is *transparent*: to understand *why* it did something, we can just look at its beliefs and its reasoning.

There are, I think, other, less obvious reasons why the logical approach was so influential. For one thing, it is appealing to imagine that reasoning provides the basis for the decisions that *we* make. And when we reason, we seem to do so in *sentences*: when contemplating the merits of various courses of action, we might have a mental conversation with ourselves, discussing the pros and cons of each. Logic-based AI seems to reflect this idea.

## CYC: THE ULTIMATE EXPERT SYSTEM

The so-called **Cyc project** was arguably the most famous experiment in the period of knowledge-based AI. Cyc was the brainchild of Doug Lenat, a gifted AI researcher who combined outstanding scientific ability with unwavering intellectual conviction and a decided ability to persuade others to buy into his vision. Lenat rose to prominence in the 1970s with a series of impressive AI systems, which in 1977 earned him the Computers and Thought Award, the most prestigious award that can be given to a young AI scientist.

In the early 1980s, Lenat became convinced that the "Knowledge is power" doctrine had applications far beyond the construction of narrowly focused expert systems. He was convinced it provided the key to general AI—the grand dream. Here is what he wrote (with coauthor Ramanathan Guha) in 1990:[4]

> We don't believe there is any shortcut to being intelligent, any yet-to-be-discovered Maxwell's equations of thought . . . [N]o powerful formalism can obviate the need for a lot of knowledge. By knowledge, we don't just mean dry, almanac-like or highly domain-specific facts. Rather, most of what we need to know to get by in the real world is . . . too much common-sense to be included in reference books; for example, animals live for a single solid interval of time, nothing can be in two places at once, animals don't like pain . . . Perhaps the hardest truth to face, one that AI has been trying to wriggle out of for 34 years, is that there is probably no elegant, effortless way to obtain this immense knowledge base. Rather, the bulk of the effort must (at least initially) be manual entry of assertion after assertion.

And so, in the mid-1980s, Lenat and colleagues set themselves the task of creating this "immense knowledge base," and the Cyc project was born.

The ambition in the Cyc project was mind-boggling. To operate as Lenat envisaged, Cyc's knowledge base would need a complete description of "consensus reality"—the world as we understand it. Pause for a moment to reflect on this challenge. Somebody would have to explicitly tell Cyc that, for example:

- **an object dropped on planet Earth will fall to the ground and that it will stop moving when it hits the ground but that an object dropped in space will not fall;**
- **a plane that runs out of fuel will crash;**
- **people tend to die in plane crashes;**
- **it is dangerous to eat mushrooms you don't recognize;**
- **red taps usually produce hot water, while blue taps usually produce cold water;**
- **. . . and so on.**

*All* the everyday knowledge that a reasonably educated person unwittingly carries with them would need to be *explicitly* written down in Cyc's own special language and fed to the system.

Lenat estimated the project would require two hundred person years of effort, and the bulk of this was expected to be in the manual entry of knowledge—telling Cyc all about our world and our understanding of it. Lenat was optimistic that, before too long, Cyc would be able to educate itself. A system capable of educating itself in the way Lenat envisaged would imply that general AI was effectively solved. Thus, the **Cyc hypothesis** was that the problem of general AI was primarily one of knowledge and that it could be solved by a suitable knowledge-based system. The Cyc hypothesis was a bet—a high-stakes bet, but one that, if it proved successful, would have world-changing consequences.

One of the paradoxes of research funding is that, sometimes, it is the absurdly ambitious ideas that win out. Indeed, some research funding agencies go out of their way to encourage world-vaulting ambition over safe but plodding proposals. Perhaps this was the case with Cyc. In any case, in 1984, Cyc received funding from the Microelectronics and Computer Technology Corporation (MCC) in Austin, Texas, and the project was launched.

Of course, it didn't work.

The first problem was that nobody had ever tried to organize the whole knowledge of human consensus reality before—where on earth do you *begin*? For a start, you need to agree on all the vocabulary that you are going to use and how all the terms you use relate to one another. This problem—defining your basic terms and concepts, and organizing your knowledge around them, goes by the grand name of **ontological engineering,** and the ontological engineering challenge posed by Cyc was far greater than any other project that had been attempted previously. Lenat and colleagues rapidly discovered that their original ideas about how to structure the knowledge that Cyc would use and the way in which this knowledge would be captured were simply too naive and imprecise, and some way into the project, they found they had to start again.

Despite these setbacks, a decade into the project, Lenat was still full of cheerful optimism, and in April 1994, his optimism caught the attention of Vaughan Pratt, a computer science professor at Stanford University.[5] Pratt is one of computing's leading theoreticians, used to thinking about the fundamental nature of computing using the precise and pedantic language of mathematics. He was intrigued by a presentation on Cyc and asked for a demo. Lenat agreed, and Pratt went to see a demo of Cyc on April 15, 1994.

In advance of the visit, Pratt wrote to Lenat to outline his expectations. He gave a list of the kinds of capabilities he was expecting to see, based on published scientific articles about Cyc. "I'm assuming the demo will work best if my expectations are well matched to Cyc's current capabilities," Pratt wrote. "If I arrive expecting too much I may go away disappointed, but if my expectations are set too low . . . we may spend too long on things that don't do justice to Cyc's full range of abilities." He did not receive a reply.

The demonstration itself started with some straightforward illustrations of modest but genuine technical accomplishments that Cyc was capable of—identifying some inconsistencies in a database that required some reasoning on behalf of Cyc. So far, so good. Then Lenat started to stretch Cyc's capabilities a little. The second demonstration involved Cyc retrieving images according to requirements that were written in ordinary English. The query "someone relaxing" resulted in a picture of three men in beachwear, holding surfboards—Cyc had correctly made a link between surfboards, surfing, and relaxing. Pratt scribbled down the chain of reasoning that Cyc took to get to this link. It required nearly twenty rules, involving some that seem slightly strange to us—"All mammals are vertebrates" was one of the rules required to get there. (The version of Cyc that Pratt saw had half a million rules.)

Pratt then wanted to explore one of the most central features of Cyc: its practical knowledge of our world. For example, Pratt asked whether Cyc knew that bread was food. His host translated the query into the rule language used by Cyc. "True," responded Cyc. "Does Cyc consider bread to be a drink?" asked Pratt. This time, Cyc got stuck. Lenat tried telling it explicitly that bread is not a drink. It still didn't work: "After a bit of fiddling we dropped this question," Pratt reported. They went on. Cyc seemed to know that various activities caused death, but not that starvation was a cause of death. In fact, Cyc didn't seem to know anything about starvation. Pratt went on to explore questions about planets, the sky, and cars, but it rapidly became clear that Cyc's knowledge was sketchy and unpredictable. For example, it didn't know that the sky was blue or that cars typically had four wheels.

Based on his expectations raised by Lenat's presentation,

Pratt had prepared a list of more than a hundred questions to ask Cyc, which he hoped would start to explore the extent of Cyc's common-sense understanding of our world. For example:

- **If Tom is 3 inches taller than Dick, and Dick is 2 inches taller than Harry, how much taller is Tom than Harry?**
- **Can two siblings each be taller than the other?**
- **Which is wetter, land or sea?**
- **Can a car drive backward? Can a plane fly backward?**
- **How long can people go without air?**

These are all pretty basic questions to ask about our everyday world, but they could not be meaningfully asked of or answered by Cyc. Reflecting on his experience, Pratt was careful with his critique of Cyc. Perhaps Cyc had made some progress toward the goal of general intelligence, he speculated; the problem was, it was impossible to tell *how far*, because Cyc's knowledge was so patchy and unevenly distributed.

If we ignore the inflated expectations, then we can see that Cyc taught us a lot about the development and organization of large knowledge-based systems. And to be strictly accurate, the Cyc hypothesis—that general AI is essentially a problem of knowledge, which can be solved via a suitable knowledge-based system—has been neither proved nor disproved yet. The fact that Cyc didn't deliver general AI doesn't demonstrate that the hypothesis was false, merely that this particular approach didn't work. It is conceivable that a different attempt to tackle general AI through knowledge-based approaches *might* deliver the goods.

In some ways, Cyc was just ahead of its time. Three decades after the Cyc project began, Google announced the **knowledge graph**—a large knowledge base, which Google use to augment their search services. The knowledge graph has a vast array of facts about real-world entities (places, people, movies, books, events), which are used to enrich the search results that Google finds. When you type in a query to Google, it typically contains names and other terms that refer to real things in the world. For example, suppose you search Google with the query "Madonna." A simple web search would respond with web pages that contain the word *Madonna*. But a search engine can be much more helpful if it understands that the character string "Madonna" refers to a popular singer (real name: Madonna Louise Ciccone). So if you search for "Madonna" on Google, you will find that the response for your query includes an array of information about the singer, which will answer most routine questions that people ask about her (date and place of birth, children, most popular recordings, and so on). One key difference between Cyc and the Google knowledge graph is that knowledge in the knowledge graph is not hand-coded but is automatically extracted from web pages such as Wikipedia—in 2017, it was claimed the system contained about seventy billion facts about five hundred million entities. Of course, the knowledge graph does not aspire to general intelligence—and it isn't clear to what extent it involves actual reasoning of the kind that was so central to the knowledge-based system's view of the world. But nevertheless, I think there is some Cyc DNA in the knowledge graph.

However we might try to justify it retrospectively, the sad fact is that Cyc's main role in AI history is as an extreme example of AI hype, which very publicly failed to live up to the grand predictions that were made for it.

## CRACKS APPEAR

Like so many versions of AI that are beautiful in theory, knowledge-based AI proved to be limited in practice. The approach struggled even with some reasoning tasks that seem absurdly trivial to us. Consider the task of **common-sense reasoning,** one classic example of which is given by following scenario:[6]

> **You are told Tweety is a bird, so you conclude Tweety can fly. Later, though, you are told that Tweety is a penguin, so you retract your earlier conclusion.**

At first sight, it looks like this problem ought to be easy to capture in logic. It looks, in fact, very much like the syllogisms that we saw earlier should do the job—as long as our AI system had the knowledge "If $x$ is a bird, then $x$ can fly," then given the information that "$x$ is a bird," it should be able to deduce that "$x$ can fly." Well, so far, so good. The difficulty comes with what happens next, when we are told that Tweety is a penguin. Then we need to retract—take back—our earlier conclusion that Tweety can fly. But logic cannot cope with this. In logic, adding more information never eliminates any of the conclusions you obtained earlier. But that is precisely what is going on here: the additional information ("Tweety is a penguin") causes us to eliminate our earlier conclusion ("Tweety can fly").

Another problem in common-sense reasoning arises when we encounter contradictions. Here is a standard example from the literature:[7]

> **Quakers are pacifists;**
>
> **Republicans are not pacifists;**
>
> **Nixon is a Republican and a Quaker.**

Try to capture this scenario in logic and a disaster ensues, because we end up concluding that Nixon both is and is not a pacifist—a contradiction. Logic fails utterly in the presence of such contradictions: it cannot cope, and it can tell us nothing useful at all. Yet this is the kind of contradictory situation we all encounter every day of our lives. We are told that taxes are good, and we are told that taxes are bad; we are told that wine is good for us and that wine is bad for us; and so on. It's ubiquitous. The problem once again is that we are trying to use logic for something it was not intended for—in mathematics, if you encounter a contradiction, then that means you made a mistake.

These problems seem almost comically trivial, but they were major research challenges for knowledge-based AI in the late 1980s—they attracted some of the smartest people in the field. And they were never really solved.

It also turned out to be harder to build and deploy successful expert systems than it first appeared. The main difficulty was what became known as the **knowledge elicitation** problem. Put simply, this is the problem of extracting knowledge from human experts and encoding it in the form of rules. Human experts often find it hard to articulate the expertise they have— the fact that they are good at something does not mean that they can tell you how they actually do it. And human experts, it transpired, were not necessarily all that eager to share their expertise. After all, if your company had a program that could do what you do, why would they keep you? Concerns about AI replacing people are nothing new.

By the end of the 1980s, the expert systems boom was over. The technology of knowledge-based systems could not be said to have failed, because many successful expert systems were built in this period, and many more have been built since. But once again, it seemed, the reality of what AI had actually produced had not lived up to the hype.

# 4

## Robots and Rationality

IN HIS 1962 book, *The Structure of Scientific Revolutions*, the philosopher Thomas Kuhn argued that, as scientific understanding advances, there will be times when established scientific orthodoxy can no longer hold up under the strain of manifest failures. At such times of crisis, he argued, a new orthodoxy will emerge and replace the established order: the scientific paradigm will change. By the late 1980s, the boom days of expert systems were over, and another AI crisis was looming. Once again, the AI community was criticized for overselling ideas, promising too much, and delivering too little. This time, the paradigm being questioned was not just the "Knowledge is power" doctrine that had driven the expert systems boom but the basic assumptions that had underpinned AI since the 1950s, symbolic AI in particular. The fiercest critics of AI in the late 1980s, though, were not outsiders but came from within the field itself.

The most eloquent and influential critic of the prevailing AI paradigm was the roboticist Rodney Brooks, who was born in Australia in 1954. Brooks's main interest was in building robots that could carry out useful tasks in the real world. Throughout the early 1980s, he began to be frustrated with the then prevailing idea that the key to building such robots was to encode knowledge about the world in a form that could be used by the robot as the basis for reasoning and decision-making. He took up a faculty position at MIT in the mid-1980s and began his campaign to rethink AI at its most fundamental level.

## THE BROOKSIAN REVOLUTION

To understand Brooks's arguments, it is helpful to return to the Blocks World. Recall that the Blocks World is a simulated domain consisting of a tabletop on which are stacked a number of different objects—the task is to rearrange the objects in certain specified ways. At first sight, the Blocks World seems perfectly reasonable as a proving ground for AI techniques: it sounds like a warehouse environment, and I daresay exactly this point has been made in many grant proposals over the years. But for Brooks, and those that came to adopt his ideas, the Blocks World was bogus for the simple reason that it is *simulated,* and the simulation glosses over everything that would be difficult about a task like arranging blocks in the real world. A system that can solve problems in the Blocks World, however smart it might appear to be, would be of no value in a warehouse, because the *real* difficulty in the physical world comes from dealing with issues like perception, which are completely ignored in the Blocks World: it became a symbol of all that was wrong and intellectually bankrupt about the AI orthodoxy of the 1970s and 1980s. (This did not stop research into the Blocks World, however: you can still regularly find research papers using it to the present day; I confess to have written some myself.)

Brooks had become convinced that meaningful progress in AI could only be achieved with systems that were **situated** in the real world: that is, systems that were directly in some environment, perceiving it and acting upon it. He argued that intelligent behavior can be generated without explicit knowledge and reasoning of the kind promoted by knowledge-based AI in general and logic-based AI in particular, and he suggested instead that intelligence is an **emergent property** that arises from the interaction of an entity in its environment. The point here is that, when we contemplate *human* intelligence, we tend to focus on its more glamorous and tangible aspects: reasoning, for example, or problem solving, or playing chess. Reasoning and problem solving might have a role in intelligent behavior, but Brooks and others argued that they were not the right *starting point* from which to build AI.[1]

Brooks also took issue with the divide-and-conquer assumption that had underpinned AI since its earliest days: the idea that progress in AI research could be made by decomposing intelligent behavior into its constituent components (reasoning, learning, perception), with no attempt to consider how these components worked together.

Finally, he pointed out the naivety of ignoring the issue of *computational effort*. In particular, he took issue with the idea that all intelligent activities must be reduced to ones such as logical reasoning, which are computationally expensive.

As a student working on AI in the late 1980s, it seemed like Brooks was challenging everything I thought I knew about my field. It felt like heresy. In 1991, a young colleague returning from a large AI conference in Australia told me, wide-eyed with excitement, about a shouting match that had developed between Ph.D. students from Stanford (McCarthy's home institute) and MIT (Brooks's). On one side, there was established tradition: logic, knowledge representation, and reasoning. On the other, the outspoken, disrespectful adherents of a new AI movement—not just turning their backs on hallowed tradition but loudly ridiculing it.

While Brooks was probably the highest-profile advocate of

the new direction, he was by no means alone. Many other researchers were reaching similar conclusions, and while they did not necessarily agree on the smaller details, there were a number of commonly recurring themes in their different approaches.

The most important was the idea that knowledge and reasoning were deposed from their role at the heart of AI. McCarthy's vision of an AI system that maintained a central symbolic, logical model of its environment (as in figure 5), around which all the activities of intelligence orbited, was firmly rejected. Some moderate voices argued that reasoning and representation still had a role to play, although perhaps not a *leading* role, but more extreme voices rejected them completely.

It is worth exploring this point in a little more detail. Remember that the McCarthy view of logical AI assumes that an AI system will continually follow a particular loop: perceiving its environment, reasoning about what to do, and then acting. But in a system that operates in this way, the system is *decoupled* from the environment.

Take a second to stop reading this book, and look around. You may be in an airport departure lounge, a coffee shop, on a train, in your home, or lying by a river in the sunshine. As you look around, you are not *disconnected* from your environment and the changes that the environment is undergoing. You are *in the moment.* Your perception—and your actions—are embedded within and in tune with your environment.

The problem is, the knowledge-based approach doesn't seem to reflect this. Knowledge-based AI assumes that an intelligent system operates through a continual *perceive-reason-act* loop, processing and interpreting the data it receives from its sensors; using this perceptual information to update its beliefs; reasoning about what to do; performing the action it then selects; and starting its decision loop again. But in this way, an AI system is inherently *decoupled* from its environment. In particular, if the environment changes *after* it has been observed, then it will make no difference to our knowledge-based intelligent system, which will stubbornly continue as though nothing had changed. You and I are not like that. For these reasons, another key theme at the time was the idea that there should be a close-coupled relationship between the *situation* that the system finds itself in and the *behavior* that it exhibits.

## BEHAVIORAL AI

If Brooks had been just another critic of AI, it is unlikely that his ideas would have gained much traction. After all, by the mid-1980s, the AI community was accustomed to ignoring its critics and carrying on regardless. What raised Brooks's critiques from being yet another Dreyfus-style attack was that he convincingly articulated an alternative paradigm and demonstrated it with some impressive systems in the decades that followed.

The new paradigm for AI became known as **behavioral AI** because, as we shall see, it emphasized the role of the specific individual behaviors that contribute to the overall operation of an intelligent system. The particular approach adopted by Brooks was called the **subsumption architecture,** and of all the approaches from the period, this seems to have had the most lasting impact. So let's see how the subsumption architecture can be used to build a modest but useful robotic application: a vacuum cleaning robot. (Brooks was a founder of the company iRobot, manufacturer of the popular Roomba robot vacuum cleaners, the design of which was based on his work.)[2] Our robot will be required to travel around a building, avoiding obstacles and vacuuming when it detects dirt—when the robot has a low battery or its dirt container is full, we want it to return to its docking station and shut down.

The basic methodology for the subsumption architecture requires identifying the individual component behaviors that are required for the robot. We then start to build our robot by getting it to exhibit one of the behaviors and then progressively add further behaviors. The key challenge is to think about how these behaviors are interrelated and to organize them in such a way that the robot is exhibiting the right behavior at the right time. This typically requires experimenting with the robot extensively, to ensure that the behaviors are organized in the right way.

Our vacuum cleaning robot requires six behaviors:

- **Avoid obstacles:** If I detect an obstacle, then change direction, choosing a new direction at random.

- **Shut down:** If I am at the docking station and have a low battery, then shut down.

- **Empty dirt:** If I am at the docking station and am carrying dirt, then empty dirt container.

- **Head to dock:** If the battery is low or dirt container is full, then head to docking station.

- **Vacuum:** If I detect dirt at the current location, then switch on vacuum.

- **Walk randomly:** Choose a direction at random and move in that direction.

**Figure 6:** A simple subsumption hierarchy for a robot vacuum cleaner.

The next challenge is to organize these behaviors. For this, Brooks suggested using what he called a **subsumption hierarchy**—see figure 6. The subsumption hierarchy determines the precedence for behaviors: those that appear lower in the hierarchy take precedence over those that appear farther up. Thus, obstacle avoidance is the highest priority behavior: the robot will *always* avoid obstacles if it ever encounters one. It is not difficult to see how these behaviors, organized into the hierarchy in figure 6, will solve the problem: the robot will search for dirt, and vacuum when it finds dirt, as long as it is not low on power or the dirt container is full; it will return to its docking station if the battery is low or the dirt container is full.

Although the behaviors in our vacuum cleaning robot look like rules, they are in fact much simpler. To implement them within a robot requires nothing like as much effort as logical reasoning. In fact, they can be directly implemented in the form of simple electrical circuits, and as a consequence, our robot will react to changing sensor data very quickly: it will be in tune with its environment.

In the decades that followed, Brooks built a string of influential robots, using the subsumption architecture as the basic development framework. His Genghis robot, for example, which now resides in the Smithsonian National Air and Space Museum, used fifty-seven behaviors arranged into a subsumption architecture to control a six-legged mobile robot.[3] It would have been ludicrously hard to build Genghis using knowledge-based AI techniques—if it had been possible at all. These developments propelled robotics back into the mainstream of AI, after decades on the sidelines.

## AGENT-BASED AI

At the beginning of the 1990s, I met one of the chief protagonists of the behavioral AI revolution—then something of a hero of mine. I was curious about what he really thought about the AI technologies that he was loudly rejecting—knowledge representation and reasoning, problem solving and planning. Did he *really* believe these had no place at all in the future of AI? "Of course not," he answered. "But I won't make a name for myself agreeing with the status quo." It was a depressing answer, although with hindsight, he was probably just trying to impress a naive young graduate student. But whether this professor really believed in what he was doing, others certainly did, and behavioral AI quickly became as mired in dogma as the traditions that had gone before. And before long, it began to be clear that while behavioral AI had raised important questions about the assumptions upon which AI was based, it too had severe limitations.

The problem was *it didn't scale*. If all we want to do is to build a robot to vacuum an apartment, then behavioral AI is all we need. A vacuum cleaning robot doesn't need to reason or be able to converse in English or solve complex problems. Because it doesn't need to do those things, we can build autonomous robot vacuum cleaners using the subsumption architecture (or something like it—there were lots of similar approaches at the time), and we will get a beautifully efficient solution. But while behavioral AI was very successful for some problems—mainly robotics—it provided no silver bullet for AI. It is hard to design behavioral systems with more than just a few behaviors, because understanding the possible interactions between behaviors becomes very difficult. Building systems using behavioral approaches was a black art—the only way to really know whether such a system was going to work was to try it out, and this was time-consuming, costly, and unpredictable.

Brooks was surely correct to point out that capabilities such as knowledge representation and reasoning are not the right foundations upon which to build intelligent behavior, and his robots demonstrated what could be achieved with purely behavioral approaches. But the dogmatic insistence that reasoning and knowledge representation have no role to play was, I think, a misstep. There *are* situations that naturally call for reasoning (whether strictly logical or otherwise), and to try to deny this makes no more sense than trying to build a vacuum cleaning robot that decides what to do by logical deduction.

While some proponents of the new AI took a hard-line view—anything like logical representation and reasoning were strictly verboten—others adopted a more moderate line, and it is this more moderate line that seems to have prevailed through to the present day. Moderates accepted the key lessons of behavioral AI but argued that the right solution was a *combination* of behavioral and reasoning approaches. A new direction for AI began to emerge, which took on board the key lessons of Brooks, while at the same time embracing what had previously proved to be successful in AI's reasoning and representation heritage.

Once again, the focus of activity in AI began to change, away from *disembodied* AI systems like expert systems and logical reasoners, toward building **agents.** An agent was intended to be an AI system that was "complete" in the sense that it was a self-contained, autonomous entity, situated in some environment and carrying out some specific task on behalf of a user. An agent was supposed to provide a complete, integrated set of capabilities, rather than just some isolated disembodied capability like logical reasoning. By focusing on building *complete* intelligent agents rather than just the *components* of intelligence, it was hoped that AI could avoid the fallacy that so irked Brooks—the idea that AI can succeed by separating out the components of intelligent behavior (reasoning, learning, and so on) and developing these in isolation from one another.

The agent-based view of AI was directly influenced by behavioral AI, but softened the message. The movement began to emerge in the early 1990s. It took the community a while to agree on what they were really talking about when they talked about "agents," but by the mid-1990s, a consensus emerged that agents had to have three important capabilities. First, they had to be reactive: they had to be attuned to their environment and able to adapt their behavior appropriately when changes in the environment demanded it. Second, they had to be proactive: capable of systematically working to achieve their given task on behalf of their user. Finally, agents were social: capable of working with other agents when required. The golden age of AI had emphasized proactive behavior—planning and problem solving; while behavioral AI had emphasized the importance of being reactive—embodied in and attuned to the environment. Agent-based AI demanded both and in addition threw something new into the mix: the idea that agents would have to work with other agents, and for this, they would need *social* skills—the ability not just to communicate but to cooperate, coordinate, and negotiate with other agents in the furtherance of their tasks.

It was this latter consideration—that agents need to be *social*—that marked out the agent-based AI paradigm from those that had preceded it. With hindsight, it seems somewhat strange that it took AI so long to start seriously thinking about how AI systems might interact with each other and what issues would arise when they did so.

## HOMER: A COMPLETE AGENT

My favorite example of an agent from this time was HOMER, a simulated robot submarine, which existed in a two-dimensional "sea world."[4] HOMER was given tasks to accomplish in the sea world, which typically related to collecting packages and moving them from one location to another. HOMER is clearly a spiritual descendent of SHRDLU and shared with SHRDLU one of its key limitations—it was only a simulation. But it was considerably more sophisticated.

HOMER took instructions from a user within a limited subset of English with about an eight-hundred-word vocabulary. HOMER could plan how to achieve its instructions and could then carry out its plans, adapting them as circumstances required. To get a feel for HOMER's capabilities, let's look at some dialogues with it. The first concerns a floating log that HOMER could see:

> What is in front of you?
>
> *A log.*
>
> Do you own the log?
>
> *No, I don't.*
>
> The log belongs to you.
>
> *Oh.* (Used by HOMER to indicate it has been told something it didn't know previously.)
>
> . . .
>
> Turn away from your log.
>
> *OK, I am turning.*
>
> (Log is moved by the user.)
>
> Turn around.
>
> *OK, I'm turning.*
>
> *I've lost the log!*

This dialogue demonstrates some simple but important common-sense reasoning: HOMER remembered the log, expected to see the log when it turned around, and was surprised when it discovered that the log had disappeared.

The next scenario starts with HOMER waiting at a pier, which has a package on it: HOMER's task was to collect the package and deliver it to a barge.

Drop the package at the barge next Saturday at 9:00 p.m.

*OK.*

(HOMER generates plan.)

Are you going to the pier next Saturday?

*Yes.*

Why are you going to go to the pier?

*I'll go to the pier in order to pick up the package.*

What time are you going to pick it up?

*8:56 p.m.*

Where will the package be next Sunday?

*At the barge.*

Will the package be at the pier a week from now?

*No.*

Here we see HOMER demonstrating some common-sense understanding of time and how its actions affect its environment— that after it has dropped off the package at the barge, the package will no longer be at the pier. It also demonstrates an understanding that its own plans will take time to accomplish—it needs to leave the pier at 8:56 p.m. in order to be at the barge for 9:00 p.m.

## AI ASSISTANTS

Although agent-based AI had its origins in robotics, many researchers quickly realized that the paradigm of agent-based AI had useful applications in the software world. There was no claim that this was general AI: the idea was that **software agents** could be built to do useful tasks on our behalf. Software agents operated in software environments, such as desktop computers and the internet. The big idea was to have AI-powered software agents working alongside us as assistants on routine everyday tasks like processing emails and surfing the web. The use of software agents in this way represented a completely different mode of human-computer interaction from what had come before. When we use an application like Microsoft Word or Internet Explorer, the application takes a passive, purely responsive role. These applications never take control or take the initiative. When Microsoft Word does something, it does it because you selected a menu item or clicked on a button. There is only one agent in the interaction between you and Microsoft Word, and that agent is you.

The **agent-based interface** changed that. Instead of the computer passively waiting to be told what to do, an agent would take an active role, in the same way that a human collaborator would. The agent would *work with you* as an assistant, actively cooperating with you to do whatever it was that you wanted to do. By the mid-1990s, spurred on by the rapid expansion of the World Wide Web, interest in software agents grew rapidly.

The title of a widely read article of the time, published by Belgian-born MIT Media Lab professor Pattie Maes, captured the zeitgeist: "Agents That Reduce Work and Information Overload."[5] The article described a number of prototype agents developed in Pattie's lab—agents for email management, meeting scheduling, filtering news, and music recommendation. The email assistant, for example, would observe a user's behavior when receiving an email (read the email immediately, file it, immediately delete it, and so on) and, using a machine learning algorithm, would try to predict what the user would do when a new email arrived. When the agent was sufficiently confident in its predictions, then it would start to take the initiative and process the email according to its prediction.

Two decades would pass before agents became a practical reality, but they did, and there is a good chance that you use one every day. In 2010, an app called Siri was launched for the Apple iPhone. Siri had been developed at SRI International—

the same institute that had developed SHAKEY three decades earlier. It was a direct descendent of the work on software agents from the 1990s and was envisaged as a software agent that users could interact with in natural language and that could carry out simple tasks on their behalf. Other mass-market software agents rapidly followed: Amazon's Alexa, Google's Assistant, and Microsoft's Cortana are all realizations of the same vision. They all trace their heritage to agent-based AI. They could not, realistically, have been built in the 1990s, because the hardware available at the time was not up to the task. To make them viable, they needed the computer power that only became available on mobile devices in the second decade of this century.

## ACTING RATIONALLY

The agent paradigm provided yet another way of thinking about AI: *building agents that can act effectively on our behalf.* But this raised an intriguing question. The Turing test established the idea that the goal of AI was to produce behavior that was *indistinguishable from that of humans.* But if we want agents to act on our behalf and do the best for us, then whether they make *the same choices that a human would make* is irrelevant. Surely what we really want is for them to make *good* choices— the best choices possible. The goal of AI thus began to shift from building agents that make *human* choices to agents that make *optimal* choices.

The theory of optimal decision-making that underpins most work in AI goes back to the 1940s, and the work of John von Neumann—the same John von Neumann whom we met in chapter 1, who did seminal work on the design of the earliest computers. Along with his colleague Oskar Morgenstern, he developed a mathematical theory of rational decision-making, which remains a cornerstone of economic theory to the present day. This theory showed how the problem of making a rational choice could be reduced to a mathematical calculation.[6] In agent-based AI, the idea was that the agent would use their theory to make optimal decisions on your behalf.

The starting point of their theory is your **preferences.** If your agent is to act on your behalf, then it needs to know what your wishes are. You then want the agent to act in order to bring about your preferred choices as best it can. So how do we give an agent our preferences? Suppose your agent has to choose between getting an apple, orange, or pear. If your agent is going to do its best for you, then it needs to know your desires with respect to these outcomes. For example, your preferences might be the following:

> **Oranges are preferred to pears;**
>
> **pears are preferred to apples.**

In this case, if your agent was given a choice between an apple and an orange, and chose an orange, you'd be happy—if it gave you an apple, you would be disappointed. This is a simple example of a **preference relation.** Your preference relation describes how you rank every pair of alternative outcomes. Von Neumann and Morgenstern required preference relations to satisfy certain basic requirements of consistency. For example, suppose you claimed your preferences were as follows:

> **Oranges are preferred to pears;**
>
> **pears are preferred to apples;**
>
> **apples are preferred to oranges.**

Your preferences here are rather odd, because the fact that you prefer oranges to pears and pears to apples would lead me to conclude you preferred oranges above apples, which contradicts the last statement. Your preferences are therefore inconsistent.

It would be impossible for an agent given such preferences to make a good decision for you.

Their next step is to see that consistent preferences can be given a *numeric* representation, using what are called **utilities.** The basic idea of utilities is that each possible outcome is associated with a number: the larger the number, the more preferred the outcome. For example, we can capture the preferences in the first example above by assigning the utility of an orange to be 3, the utility of a pear to be 2, and the utility of an apple to be 1. Since 3 is bigger than 2 and 2 is bigger than 1, these utilities correctly capture our first preference relation. Equally well, we could have chosen utilities so that oranges have value 10, pears have value 9, and apples have value 0. The *magnitude* of the values doesn't matter in this case: all that is important is the *ordering* of outcomes that is induced by the utility values. Crucially, it is *only* possible to represent preferences via numeric utility values if they satisfy the consistency constraints—see if you can assign numeric values to apples, oranges, and pears in order to represent the example with inconsistent preferences above!

The sole purpose of using utility values to represent preferences is that it reduces the problem of making the best choice to a mathematical calculation. Our agent chooses an action whose outcome maximizes utility on our behalf; which is the same as saying that it chooses an action in order to bring about our most preferred outcome. Problems like this are called *optimization problems,* and they have been extensively studied in mathematics.

Unfortunately, most choices are trickier than this because they involve uncertainty. Settings of **choice under uncertainty** deal with scenarios where actions have multiple possible outcomes, and all we know about these outcomes is the *probability* that each will result.

To understand what I mean by this, let's look at a scenario in which your agent has to make a choice between two options.[7] Here is the scenario:

- **Option 1:** A fair coin is tossed. If it comes up heads, your agent is given $4. If it comes up tails, your agent is given $3.

- **Option 2:** A fair coin is tossed. If it comes up heads, your agent is given $6. If it comes up tails, your agent is given nothing.

Which option should your agent choose? I claim that Option 1 is a better choice. But why, exactly, is it better?

To understand why this is, we need a concept called **expected utility**. The expected utility of a scenario is the utility that would be received *on average* from that scenario.

So consider Option 1. The coin we are tossing is fair (not weighted to either heads or tails), and so we would expect heads and tails to come up, on average, an equal number of times—heads half the time, tails half the time. So half the time, your agent would receive $4, and half the time, it would receive $3. On average, therefore, the amount you would expect to earn from Option 1 would therefore be $(0.5 \times \$4) + (0.5 \times \$3) = \$3.50$; this is the expected utility of the option.

Of course, if your agent chose Option 1, then *in practice*, it would never actually receive $3.50; but if you had the opportunity to make this choice enough times, and you always chose Option 1, then on average you would receive $3.50 each time you made the choice.

Following the same reasoning, the expected utility of Option 2 is $(0.5 \times \$6) + (0.5 \times \$0) = \$3$, so on average choosing Option 2 would give you $3.

Now, the basic principle of rational choice in Von Neumann

and Morgenstern's theory says that a rational agent would make a choice **maximizing expected utility.** In this case, the choice that maximizes expected utility would be Option 1, since this gives the expected utility of $3.50 against the expected utility of $3 with Option 2.

Note that Option 2 offers the tantalizing possibility of getting $6, which is more than would be received with any outcome associated with Option 1; but this attractive possibility has to be weighed against the equally likely possibility of getting nothing in Option 2, which is why the expected utility of Option 1 is larger.

The idea of maximizing expected utility is often grossly misunderstood. Some people find the idea of reducing human preferences and choices to a mathematical calculation distasteful. This distaste often arises from the mistaken belief that utilities are money or that utility theory is in some sense selfish (since presumably an agent that maximizes expected utility must be acting only for itself). But utilities are nothing more than a numeric way of capturing preferences: Von Neumann and Morgenstern's theory is completely neutral with respect to what an individual's preferences are or should be. The theory copes equally well with the preferences of angels and devils. If all you care about is other people, then that's fine: if your altruism is captured in your preferences, utility theory will work for you just as well as it does for the most selfish person in the world.

By the 1990s, the idea of AI as the paradigm of building agents that would act rationally on our behalf, with rationality defined according to the Von Neumann and Morgenstern model, had become the new orthodoxy in AI and remains so today:[8] if there is any common theme that unites the various strands of contemporary AI, it is this. Inside almost all AI systems today, there is a numeric utility model, representing the preferences of the user, and the system will try to maximize expected utility according to this model—to act rationally on behalf of the user.

## COPING WITH UNCERTAINTY

One long-term problem in AI, which became much more crisply defined in the 1990s, was that of dealing with uncertainty. Any realistic AI system has to deal with uncertainty, and sometimes a lot of it. To pick an example, a driverless car obtains streams of data from its sensors, but sensors are not perfect. For example, there is always a chance that a range finder will simply be wrong when it says, "No obstacle." The information the range finder has is not useless—it has some value—but we can't just assume it is correct. So how should we make use of it, taking into account the possibility of error?

Many ad hoc schemes for dealing with uncertainty were invented and reinvented throughout the history of AI, but by the 1990s, one approach had come to dominate. The approach is called **Bayesian inference.** Bayesian inference was invented by an eighteenth-century British mathematician, the Reverend Thomas Bayes. He formulated a version of a technique that we now call **Bayes's theorem** in his honor. It is concerned with how we should rationally adjust our beliefs in the presence of new information. In the case of our driverless car example, the beliefs relate to whether there is an obstacle in front of us; the new information is the sensor data.

Apart from anything else, Bayes's theorem is interesting because it highlights how poorly people cope with cognitive decisions involving uncertainty. To better understand this, consider the following scenario (the scenario is a pretty standard one, invented long before the 2020 pandemic):

**A deadly new flu virus infects one in every thousand people.**
**A test for the flu is developed, which is 99 percent accurate.**

**On a whim you take the test, and it comes out positive. How concerned should you be?**

After the test came back positive, I think it is a safe bet that most people would be *extremely* concerned. After all, the test is *99 percent accurate*! So if I asked what the probability was that you had the flu after the positive test, I suspect most people would say 0.99 (corresponding to the accuracy of the test).

In fact, this answer is hopelessly wrong. You would only have about a *one in ten* chance of having the flu. So what is going on here?

Imagine that we select 1,000 people at random and give them the flu test. We know that only about 1 person in this 1,000 will actually have the flu, so let's assume that in our test, this is indeed the case: 1 person has the flu, and 999 don't.

First, let's consider the poor soul who has the flu. Since the test is 99 percent accurate, it will correctly identify someone who actually has the flu 99 percent of the time. So we can expect this test to come out positive (with probability 0.99).

Now think about the lucky 999 souls who *don't* have the flu. Again, the test is 99 percent accurate, so it will only misdiagnose someone who doesn't have the flu about 1 time in every 100 tests. But we are testing 999 people who don't have the flu; so we can expect something like 9 or 10 of those tests to come back positive. In other words, about 9 or 10 of those people can be expected to test positive for the flu *even though they don't have it*.

So if we test 1,000 people for the flu, we can expect about 10 or 11 of those tests to come back positive; but we can also expect that only one of the people who tests positive actually has the flu.

In short, since so few people do have the flu there will be far more *false positives* than *true positives*. (This, incidentally, is one reason why doctors don't like to rely on a single test to make a diagnosis.)

Let's look at an example of how Bayesian reasoning can be used in robotics. Let's suppose we have a robot that is exploring some unknown territory—a distant planet or a building that has been devastated by an earthquake. We want our robot to explore the new territory and construct a map of it. The robot can perceive its environment through its sensors, but there is a catch: the sensors are noisy. Thus, when the robot makes an observation and the sensors say, "There is an obstacle in this location," they may be right or they may be wrong. We don't know for sure. If our robot just assumes its sensor data is always correct, then at some point it will make a decision based on incorrect information and crash into an obstacle.

Bayes's theorem here is used as follows. Just as in the test for the flu, we can use the probability that the sensor reading is correct to update our beliefs that there is an obstacle at the relevant location. By making multiple observations, we can progressively refine our map of the environment.[9] And over time, we become increasingly confident about where the obstacles are.

Bayes's theorem is important because it gives us the right way of handling imperfect data: we neither discard the data nor accept it without question. Instead, we use it to update our probabilistic beliefs about how the world is.

## AI REACHES MATURITY

By the end of the 1990s, the agent paradigm had become established as the orthodoxy in AI: we build agents and delegate our preferences to them; these agents act rationally on our behalf to carry them out, using rational decision-making as exemplified by Von Neumann and Morgenstern's expected utility theory; and these agents rationally manage their beliefs about the world using Bayesian reasoning. This was not general AI, and it didn't give any road map for how to get to general AI. But by the end of the 1990s, the increasing acceptance of these tools led to an important change in the perception of AI within the AI community itself. For the first time, it really felt like we were not just groping in the dark, desperately clutching onto whatever we found: we had a well-established scientific basis for our field, one that was firmly grounded in respected and proven techniques from probability theory and the theory of rational decision-making.

Two achievements in this period signaled the maturity of the discipline. The first made headlines around the world; the second, equally if not more important, is unknown to all but AI insiders.

The headline breakthrough was made by IBM, who, in 1997, were able to show that an AI system, by the name of DeepBlue, was able to beat Russian grand master Garry Kasparov in the game of chess. DeepBlue took its first match from Kasparov in February 1996 in a six-game tournament, but Kasparov won overall, four games to two. An upgraded version of the system played Kasparov just over a year later, and this time DeepBlue defeated Kasparov overall. It seems Kasparov was very unhappy about it at the time, apparently suspecting IBM of cheating, but he has since enjoyed a good sideline to his brilliant chess career by speaking about the experience. From that point on, chess was, for all intents and purposes, a solved game: AI systems existed that could reliably beat all but the very best players.

While you may well have heard of DeepBlue's victory over Kasparov, I think it is unlikely that you will have heard of the second major achievement of the time, although its ramifications are probably more profound. You may recall from chapter 2 that certain computational problems are intrinsically hard—NP-complete, to use the technical term—and that many problems of interest in AI fall into this category. By the early 1990s, it was beginning to be clear that progress on algorithms for NP-complete problems was such that this no longer represented the fundamental barrier that it had appeared two decades before.[10] The first problem shown to be NP-complete was called SAT (short for *satisfiability*). This is the problem of checking whether simple logical expressions are consistent—whether there is any way they could be true. SAT is the most fundamental of all NP-complete problems: if you find an efficient way to solve SAT, then you have also found a way to solve *all* NP-complete problems. By the end of the 1990s, *SAT solvers*—programs to solve SAT problems—were sufficiently powerful that they began to be used on industrial-scale problems. At the time of writing, SAT solvers are so efficient that they are now routinely used throughout computing—they are just another tool that we call on when faced with NP-complete problems. This doesn't mean that NP-complete problems can now always be solved neatly: there will always be cases that bring even the best SAT solvers to their knees. But we are no longer afraid of NP-completeness, and this is one of the major unsung achievements of AI over the past four decades.

For all its newfound respectability, not everyone was happy about what mainstream AI had become by the end of the 1990s. In July 2000, I was at a conference in Boston, watching a presentation by one of the bright young stars of the new AI. I was sitting next to a seasoned AI veteran—someone who had been in AI since the golden age, a contemporary of McCarthy and Minsky. He was contemptuous. "Is this what passes for AI nowadays?" he asked. "Where did the magic go?" And I could see where he was coming from: a career in AI now demanded a background not in philosophy or cognitive science or logic but in probability, statistics, and economics. It doesn't seem as, well, *poetic*, does it? But the fact is, it worked.

AI had changed direction again, but this time, the future

seemed much more settled. Had I been writing this book in the year 2000, I would have confidently predicted that this would be the future of AI for the rest of my career. There would be no drama: we would use these tools and that, with them, progress would be slow but steady. I had no inkling that, just around the corner, dramatic new developments were about to shake AI to its core once again.

# 5

## Deep Breakthroughs

IN JANUARY 2014, something unprecedented happened in the UK technology industry. Google acquired a small company in a deal that, while unremarkable by the otherworldly standards of Silicon Valley, was extraordinary by the standards of the UK's rather modest computer technology sector. The company they acquired was DeepMind, a start-up company which at the time employed fewer than twenty-five people, for the reported sum of $650 million.[1] At the time of acquisition, it looked from the outside as though DeepMind had no products, technology, or business plan. They were virtually unknown, even within the specialist area in which they had chosen to operate: AI.

The acquisition of this tiny AI company for a huge sum made headlines—the world wanted to know who this mystery outfit were and why Google thought an unknown company could possibly be worth so much.

Artificial intelligence was suddenly big news—and big business. Interest in AI exploded. The press noticed the buzz, and stories about AI began to appear in the media daily. Governments across the globe also noticed and started to ask how they should respond; a string of national AI initiatives quickly followed. Technology companies scrambled to avoid being left behind, and an unprecedented wave of investment followed. While DeepMind was the highest-profile AI acquisition, there were many others. In 2015, Uber acquired no fewer than forty researchers from Carnegie Mellon University's machine learning lab in a single deal.

In less than a decade, AI had been transformed from a quiet backwater of computing into the hottest and most hyped area of science. The sudden sea change in attitudes to AI was driven by rapid progress in one core AI technology: machine learning. Machine learning is a subfield of AI, but for much of the last sixty years, it had evolved on a separate path, and as we will see in this chapter, the relationship between AI and its suddenly glamorous offspring has at times been strained.

In this chapter, we will hear how the twenty-first-century machine learning revolution happened. We'll begin by briefly reviewing what machine learning is and then look at how one particular approach to machine learning—*neural networks*—came to dominate. Like the story of AI itself, the story of neural networks is a troubled one: there have been two "neural net winters," and as recently as the turn of the century, many in AI regarded neural networks as a dead or dying field. But neural nets ultimately triumphed, and the new idea driving their resurgence is a technique called **deep learning.** Deep learning is the core technology of DeepMind. I will tell you the DeepMind story and how the systems that DeepMind built attracted global adulation. But while deep learning is a powerful and important technique, it isn't the end of the story for AI, so just as we did with other AI technologies, we'll discuss its limitations in detail too.

## MACHINE LEARNING, BRIEFLY

The goal of machine learning is to have programs that can compute a desired output from a given input, *without being given an explicit recipe for how to do this.* An example is in order. One classic application of machine learning is text recognition: taking handwritten text and transcribing it. Here, the input is a picture of the handwritten text; the desired output is the string of characters represented by the handwritten text.

Text recognition is hard, as any postal worker will tell you. We all write differently, and many of us write unclearly; we use pens that leak ink onto the paper; and the paper itself becomes dirty and battered. Returning to the discussion in chapter 2, text recognition is an example of a problem for which we don't know how to come up with an appropriate recipe. It isn't like playing board games, where we have recipes that work in principle but need heuristics to make them practical; we just don't know what a recipe for text recognition might be. We need something else entirely—which is where machine learning comes in.

A machine learning program for text recognition would typically be **trained** by giving it many examples of handwritten characters, with each example labeled with the actual text that was written. Figure 7 illustrates this.

The type of machine learning we have just described is called **supervised learning,** and it illustrates a crucially important point: *machine learning needs data.* Lots and

| Input | Output |
|-------|--------|
| 8 | 8 |
| 3 | 3 |
| 2 | 2 |
| 1 | 1 |
| 4 | 4 |
| 8 | 8 |
| 2 | 2 |
| 1 | 1 |
| 9 | 9 |
| 8 | 8 |
| 9 | ? |

**Figure 7:** Training data for a machine learning program to recognize handwritten characters (in this case, numbers). The goal is that the program will be able to identify handwritten numbers on its own.

lots of data. In fact, as we will see, the provision of carefully curated sets of training data was crucial to the current success of machine learning.

When we train a machine learning program, we have to be very careful about the training data that we use. First, we can usually only train the program with a tiny fraction of the overall space of inputs and outputs. In our handwriting example, we can't show the program all possible handwritten characters— that's impossible. If we *could* train the program with the complete set of possible inputs, then there would be no need for any clever machine learning techniques: our program could just remember each input and corresponding desired output. Whenever it was then presented with an input, all it would have to do would be to look up the corresponding output. This is not machine learning. So a program will have to be trained using only a small part of the overall set of possible inputs and outputs. But if the training data set is too small, then the program may not have enough information to learn the desired mapping from inputs to outputs.

Another fundamental problem with training data is called **feature extraction.** Suppose you are working for a bank, which wants a machine learning program that will learn to identify bad credit risks. The training data for your program will probably consist of lots of records of past customers, each customer record being labeled with whether that customer in fact turned out to be a good or bad risk. The customer record will typically include their name, date of birth, residential address, annual income, along with records of transactions, loans corresponding repayments, and so on. These components are called the **features** that can be used for training. But does it make sense to include *all* these features in your training data? Some of them may be completely irrelevant to whether someone is a bad credit risk. If you don't know in advance which features are going to be relevant for your problem, then you might be tempted to include everything. But there is a big problem with this, called the **curse of dimensionality:** the more features you include, the more training data you are going to have to give the program, and the more slowly the program is going to learn.

The natural response is to only include a small number of features in your training data. But this presents problems of its own. For one thing, you may accidentally omit features that are necessary for the program to be able to learn appropriately—the features that actually indicate a poor credit risk. For another, if you make a poor choice of which features to include, then you also run the risk of introducing **bias** into your program. For example, if the only feature that you decided to include for your bad-risk program was the address of the customer, then this is likely to lead to the program learning to discriminate against people from certain neighborhoods. The possibility that AI programs may become biased, and the problems this raises, are explored in more detail later.

In **reinforcement learning,** we don't give the program any explicit training data: it experiments by making decisions and receives feedback on those decisions as to whether they were good or bad. For example, reinforcement learning is widely used to train programs to play games. The program plays the game and gets positive feedback if it wins or negative feedback if it loses. The feedback it gets, whether positive or negative, is called the **reward.** The reward is taken into account by the program the next time it plays. If it receives a positive reward, then that makes it more likely to play the same way; a negative reward would make it less likely to do so.

A key difficulty with reinforcement learning is that in

many situations, rewards may be a long time in coming, and this makes it hard for the program to know which actions were good and which were bad. Suppose our reinforcement-learning program loses a game. What does that loss tell it—or indeed, us—about any individual move made during the game? Concluding that *all* the moves were bad would probably be an overgeneralization. But how does it and how do we know which were the bad moves? This is the **credit assignment** problem.

So far, we have said nothing about *how* a program might learn. Machine learning as a field is as old as AI itself, and just as large. Many techniques have been proposed over the past sixty years. But the recent successes of machine learning have been based around one particular technique: neural networks (usually abbreviated to *neural nets*). Neural nets are in fact one of the oldest techniques in AI—they were part of the original proposal by John McCarthy for his AI summer school in 1956. But they have seen a huge resurgence of interest this century.

Neural nets, as the name suggests, were inspired by the networks of nerve cells—**neurons**—that are found in the microstructure of the brain and nervous system. Neurons are cells that can communicate with each other in a simple way, through fibers in the brain called **axons** to other neurons via "junctions" called **synapses.** Typically, a neuron receives electrochemical signals via its synaptic connections and, depending on the signals received, will generate an output signal that will in turn be received by other neurons via their synaptic connections. Crucially, the inputs that a neuron receives are differently weighted: some inputs are more important than others, and some inputs may inhibit the neuron, preventing it from generating an output. In animal nervous systems, networks of neurons are massively interconnected: the human brain is made up of about one hundred billion neurons, and neurons in the human brain typically have thousands of connections.

The idea of neural nets in machine learning, then, is to use these kinds of structures in a computer program; after all, the human brain provides proof that neural structures can learn very effectively.

## PERCEPTRONS (NEURAL NETS VERSION 1)

The study of neural networks had its origins in the work of U.S. researchers Warren McCulloch and Walter Pitts in the 1940s. They realized that neurons could be modeled as electrical circuits—more specifically, simple logical circuits—and they used this idea to develop a straightforward but very general mathematical model of them. In the 1950s, this model was refined by Frank Rosenblatt in a neural net model that he called **perceptrons.** The **perceptron model** is significant because it was the first neural net model to actually be implemented, and is still of relevance today.

Rosenblatt's perceptron model is shown in figure 8. The oval indicates the neuron itself; the arrows going into the oval correspond to the inputs of the neuron (corresponding to its synaptic connections), and the arrow coming out to the right indicates the output of the neuron (corresponding to an axon). In the perceptron model, each input is associated with a number called its **weight:** in figure 8, the weight associated with Input 1 is $w_1$, the weight associated with Input 2 is $w_2$, and the weight associated with Input 3 is $w_3$. Each input to the neuron is either active or inactive: if an input is active, then it "stimulates" the neuron by the corresponding weight. Finally, each neuron has an **activation threshold,** which is another number (written as $T$). The idea is that if the neuron is stimulated beyond its activation threshold, $T$, then it will "fire," which means making its output active. In other words, we add together the weights of all the inputs that are active; and if the total meets or exceeds $T$, then the neuron produces an output.

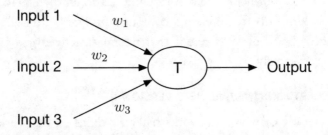

**Figure 8:** A single neural unit in Rosenblatt's perceptron model.

Of course, the neural nets that we see in nature contain many neurons and are arranged in much more complex patterns. Artificial neural networks are usually organized in **layers,** as shown in figure 9, in what is known as a **multilayer perceptron.** This network consists of nine neurons, arranged into three layers of three neurons each. Every neuron in each successive layer receives all the outputs from the layer preceding it.

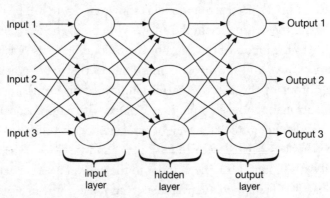

**Figure 9:** A neural net with nine neurons in three layers.

One immediate point to note is that even in this very small network, things have started to get complicated: we now have a total of twenty-seven connections between neurons, each with their own weight, and all nine neurons have their own activation threshold. Although multiple layers for neural nets were envisaged as far back as the work of McCulloch and Pitts, in Rosenblatt's time, attention was focused on networks with a single layer, for the simple reason that nobody had any idea how to train neural networks with more than one layer.

The weights associated with each connection are crucial to the operation of a neural net. In fact, that is really all a neural net breaks down into: this list of numbers. (For any reasonably sized neural network, it will be a *long* list of numbers.) Training a neural network therefore involves finding appropriate numeric weights somehow. The usual approach is to adjust the weight after each training episode, trying to make the network correctly map inputs to outputs. Rosenblatt experimented with a few different techniques for doing this and found one for a simple perceptron model, which he called an *error correction procedure*.

Nowadays, we know that Rosenblatt's approach is guaranteed to work: it will always train a program correctly, but there is one very big caveat. In 1969, Marvin Minsky and Seymour Papert published a book entitled *Perceptrons*,[2] in which they showed that there are quite dramatic limits to what single-layer perceptron networks can do. Minsky and Papert's book remains controversial even today. Theoretical results that demonstrated the fundamental limitations of *certain classes of perceptron* seem to have been taken to imply limitations for all neural network models. In particular, *multilayer* perceptrons, of the type shown in figure 9, are *not* subject to these limitations. However, at the time, nobody had any idea how to train a network with multiple layers: they were a theoretical possibility rather than a working reality. It would take two decades before the science was developed that made this possible.

Research into neural nets declined sharply at the end of the 1960s in favor of the symbolic AI approaches championed by McCarthy, Minsky, Newell, and Simon (ironically, this decline came only a few years before the onset of the AI winter that we heard about in chapter 3). In 1971, Rosenblatt died in a sailing accident, leaving the neural nets community without one of its main champions. Perhaps had he survived, the history of AI might have been different, but following his death, research into neural nets went into abeyance for more than a decade.

## CONNECTIONISM (NEURAL NETS VERSION 2)

The field of neural nets was largely dormant until a revival began in the 1980s. The revival was heralded by the publication of a two-volume book entitled *Parallel Distributed Processing* (or PDP, for short).[3] PDP provided much more general models of neurons than were provided by perceptron models, and these models in turn enabled probably the most important contribution of the new body of work: a technique called **backpropagation,** used for training multilayer neural nets. As is often the case in science, backpropagation (often called **backprop**) seems to have been invented and reinvented a number of times over the years, but it was the specific approach introduced by the PDP researchers that definitively established it.[4]

The development of backprop and the other innovations introduced by the PDP community made possible a whole slew of applications for neural nets, which went far beyond the simple demonstrations of perceptron models of twenty years earlier. Interest in neural nets exploded—but the PDP bubble proved to be short-lived. By the mid-1990s, neural net research was once more out of favor. With hindsight, we can see that the wheels came off the PDP wagon not because of any fundamental limitations of the basic ideas but for a much more prosaic reason: computers of that time were just not powerful enough to handle the new techniques. And at the same time that advances in PDP seemed to be flatlining, other areas of machine learning seemed to be making rapid progress. Mainstream interest in machine learning began to turn away from neural models once again.

## DEEP LEARNING (NEURAL NETS VERSION 3)

By around 2005, neural net research was again back in favor, and the big idea that drove the third wave of neural net research went by the name of **deep learning**.[5] I would love to tell you that there was a single key idea that characterizes deep learning, but in truth, the term refers to a collection of related ideas. Deep learning means *deep* in at least three different senses.

Of these, perhaps the most important, as the name suggests, is simply the idea of having *more layers*. Each layer can process a problem at a different level of abstraction—layers close to the input layer handle low-level concepts in the data (such as the edges in a picture), and as we move deeper into the network, we find more abstract concepts being handled.

As well as being deep in the sense of more layers, deep learning was able to enjoy the benefits of having larger numbers of neurons. A typical neural network from 1990 might only have about one hundred neurons (the human brain, you will recall, has about one hundred billion). No surprise, then, that such networks are very limited in what they can achieve. A state-of-the-art neural net from 2016 would have about one million neurons[6] (about the same number as a bee).

Finally, deep learning uses networks that are deep in the sense that the neurons themselves have many connections. In a highly connected neural network from the 1980s, each neuron might have 150 connections with other neurons. A neuron in a state-of-the-art neural network at the time of writing would have about as many connections as there are in a cat brain; a human neuron has on average about 10,000.

So deep neural networks have more layers and more, better-connected neurons. To train such networks, techniques beyond backprop were needed, and these were provided in 2006 by Geoff Hinton, a British-Canadian researcher who, more than anyone else, is identified with the deep learning movement. Hinton is a remarkable individual. He was one of the leaders of the PDP movement in the 1980s and one of the inventors of backprop. What I find personally so remarkable is that Hinton didn't lose heart when PDP research began to lose favor. He stuck with it and saw it through to its next incarnation, in the form of deep learning—for which he has received international acclaim. (Hinton is also, as it happens, the great-great-grandson of George Boole, whom we met in chapter 3 as one of the founders of modern logic; although, as Hinton has pointed out, that is probably the only thing that connects him to the logical tradition in AI.)

Deeper, bigger, more interconnected neural nets were one key ingredient in the success of deep learning; and work by Hinton and others on new techniques for training neural nets was another. But there were two further ingredients required to make deep learning a success: *data* and *computer power*.

The importance of data to machine learning can be illustrated no better than by the story of the **ImageNet** project.[7] ImageNet was the brainchild of Chinese-born researcher Fei-Fei Li. Born in Beijing in 1976, Li moved to the United States in the 1980s and studied physics and electrical engineering. She joined Stanford University in 2009 and headed the AI lab at Stanford from 2013 to 2018. Li's insight was that the entire deep learning community would benefit from having large, well-maintained data sets that would provide a common baseline against which new systems could be trained, tested, and compared. To this end, she started the ImageNet project.

ImageNet is a large online archive of images—about 14 million images at the time of writing. The images themselves are nothing more than photographs that you can download in common digital formats, such as JPEG. Crucially, though, the images have been carefully classified into 22,000 different categories, using an online thesaurus called WordNet,[8] which contains a large number of words that have been carefully arranged into categories, for example, identifying words that have the same or opposite meanings, and so on. Looking into the ImageNet archive now, I can see it has about 1,032 pictures in the category of "volcanic crater," and about 122 pictures in the category of "frisbee." The eureka moment for image classification came in 2012, when Geoff Hinton and two colleagues, Alex Krizhevsky and Ilya Sutskever, demonstrated a system called **AlexNet,** a neural net that dramatically improved performance in an international image recognition competition, based on ImageNet.[9]

The final ingredient required to make deep learning work was raw computer-processing power. Training a deep neural net requires a huge amount of computer-processing time. The work that needs to be done in training is not particularly complex— but there is an enormous amount of it.

For all their undoubted successes, deep learning and neural nets suffer from some well-publicized drawbacks.

First, the intelligence they embody is **opaque.** The expertise that a neural network has captured is embodied in the numeric weights associated with the links between neurons, and as yet, we have no way of getting at or interpreting this knowledge. A deep learning program that tells you it sees cancerous tumors in an x-ray scan cannot justify its diagnosis; a deep learning program that declines a bank loan for a customer cannot tell you why it does so. In chapter 3, we saw that expert systems like MYCIN were capable of a crude form of explanation—retracing the reasoning that was used to reach a conclusion or recommendation—but neural networks are not even capable of this. There is a lot of work under way currently to try to deal with this issue. But at present, we have no idea how to interpret the knowledge and representations that neural networks embody.

Another key problem for deep learning is that, in a subtle but very important way, neural networks are not robust. For example, it is possible to make subtle changes to images, which are undetectable to humans but which result in neural nets completely misclassifying them. Figure 10 illustrates this.[10] On the left is the original image of a panda; on the right, a doctored image. I hope you will agree that the two images appear to be the same, and in particular, they both seem to be pictures of a panda. While a neural net correctly classifies the image on the left as a panda, the image on the right is classified as a gibbon. The study of these issues is known as **adversarial machine learning**—the terminology arises from the idea that an adversary is deliberately trying to obfuscate or confuse the program.

While we might not be overly concerned if our image classification program incorrectly classified our collection of animal images, adversarial machine learning has thrown up much more disturbing examples. For example, it turns out that road signs can be altered in such a way that, while a human has no difficulty interpreting them, they are completely misunderstood by the neural nets in a driverless car. Before we can use deep learning in sensitive applications, we need to understand these problems in much more detail.

**Figure 10:** Panda or gibbon? A neural network correctly classifies image (a) as a panda. However, it is possible to adjust this image in a way that is not detectable to a human so that the same neural network classifies the resulting image (b) as a gibbon.

## DEEPMIND

The story of DeepMind, which I referred to at the start of this chapter, perfectly epitomizes the rise of deep learning. The company was founded in 2010 by Demis Hassabis, an AI researcher and computer games enthusiast, together with his school friend and entrepreneur Mustafa Suleyman, and they were joined by Shane Legg, a computational neuroscientist that Hassabis met while working at University College London.

As we read earlier, Google acquired DeepMind early in 2014; I can recall seeing stories in the press about the acquisition and starting in surprise when I saw that DeepMind were an *AI* company. It was obvious at the time of the acquisition that AI was big news again, but the idea that there was an AI company in the UK *that I had never heard of* that was worth (apparently) $650 million was utterly bewildering. Along with many others, I immediately went to the DeepMind website, but frankly, it didn't give me much more information. There were no details at all about the company's technology, products, or services. It did, however, present one rather intriguing tidbit: the publicly stated mission of DeepMind, it said, was *to solve the puzzle of intelligence.* I have already mentioned that the wildly varying fortunes of AI over the past sixty years have taught me to be wary of ambitious predictions about progress in AI: you can imagine how startled I was to see such a bold statement from a company that had just been acquired by one of the world's technology giants.

But the website offered no more detail, and I could find nobody who knew any more than I did. Most colleagues in AI regarded the announcement with skepticism, possibly tinged with a little professional jealousy. I heard little more about DeepMind until later that year, when I happened to meet my colleague Nando de Freitas. Nando is one of the world leaders in deep learning, and at the time, he was a professor alongside me at Oxford University (he later left to work with DeepMind).

He was on his way to a seminar with his students, and under his arm, he was clutching a pile of scientific papers. He was obviously excited about something. He told me, "This group in London, they've trained a program to play Atari video games from scratch."

I have to say, at first I was not impressed. Programs that can play video games are nothing new. It's the sort of challenge we might give to an undergraduate student as a project—which is what I told Nando. So he patiently explained what was going on—and then I understood why he was so excited, and it slowly began to dawn on me that we really *were* entering a new era of AI.

The Atari system that Nando referred to was the Atari 2600 game console dating from the late 1970s. The Atari 2600 was one of the first successful video game platforms: it supported video at the grand resolution of a 210 × 160 pixel grid, with up to 128 different colors; user input was through a joystick equipped with a single Fire button. The platform used plug-in cartridges for game software, and the version that DeepMind used had forty-nine games in total. They described their aim as follows:[11]

> Our goal is to create a single neural network agent that is able to successfully learn to play as many of the games as possible. The network was not provided with any game-specific information or hand-designed visual features, and was not privy to the internal state of the emulator; it learned from nothing but the video input, the [score] . . . and the set of possible actions—just as a human player would.

To understand the significance of DeepMind's achievement, it is important to understand what their program did and didn't do. Perhaps most important, *nobody told the program anything at all about the games it was playing.* If we were trying to build an Atari-playing program using knowledge-based AI, then the way we would probably proceed would be by extracting knowledge from an expert Atari player and trying to encode it using rules or some other knowledge representation scheme. (Good luck with that, if you want to try.) But DeepMind's program was given *no* knowledge about the game at all. The only information the program was given was the image that would appear on the screen and the current score of the game. That was it—the program had nothing else to go on whatsoever. What is particularly significant here is that the program was not given information such as "object $A$ is at location $(x, y)$"—any information like this would have to be somehow extracted from the raw video data *by the program itself.*

The results were remarkable.[12] The program taught itself to play using reinforcement learning: playing a game repeatedly, experimenting in each game and getting feedback, and learning which actions led to rewards versus those that didn't. The program learned to play twenty-nine of the forty-nine games at above human-level performance. With some games, it achieved superhuman levels of performance.

One game in particular attracted a lot of interest. The game of *Breakout* was one of the first video games to be developed in the 1970s: it involves the player controlling a "bat," which is used to bounce a "ball" up to a wall, which is made up of colored "bricks." Every time the ball hits a brick, the brick is destroyed, and the goal is to destroy the whole wall as quickly as possible. Figure 11 shows the program at an early stage of learning to play (after

**Figure 11:** DeepMind's Atari player missing the ball at an early stage of learning to play *Breakout.*

it has played the game about a hundred times)—at this stage, it misses the ball frequently.

After a few hundred more training rounds, the program becomes expert: it doesn't *ever* miss the ball. And then something remarkable happened. The program learned that the most efficient way to accumulate points was to "drill" a hole down the side of the wall so that the ball was above the wall: the ball would then quickly bounce between the wall and the top barrier, without the player having to do anything (figure 12). This behavior was not anticipated by DeepMind's engineers: it was autonomously learned by the program. The video of the game is readily available

**Figure 12:** Eventually the program learns that the best way to quickly accumulate a good score is to "drill" a hole through the wall so that the ball bounces above it. Nobody told the program to do this, and this behavior took the developers completely by surprise.

online: I have used it in my lectures dozens of times. Every time I show the video to a new audience, there is an audible gasp of amazement as the audience understands what the program had learned to do.

If their Atari-playing program was the only thing that Deep-Mind had ever accomplished, then they would have earned a respectable place in AI history. But the company followed it up with a further series of successes.

The most famous of these—and, at the time of writing, probably still the most famous AI system built to date—was called **AlphaGo.** It was a program to play the ancient Chinese board game Go.

Go is an intriguing target for AI. The rules of Go are *extremely* simple—much simpler than chess, for example. And yet, in 2015, Go-playing programs were well below the level of human expert performance. So why was Go such a difficult target? The answer is simply that the game is *big*. The board is a 19 × 19 grid, giving a total of 361 places where pieces may be laid; chess is played on an 8 × 8 grid, with therefore only 64 places for pieces. As we saw in chapter 2, the branching factor for Go (the average number of moves available to a player at any given point in the game) is about 250, while chess has a branching factor of about 35. In other words, *Go is much larger than chess in terms of its board size and branching factor.* And games of Go can last for a long time: 150 moves in one game is common.

AlphaGo used two neural networks: one, the **value network,** was solely concerned with estimating how good a given board position was, while another, the **policy network,** made recommendations about which move to make, based on a current board position.[13] The policy network contained thirteen layers and was trained by using supervised learning first, where the training data was examples of expert games played by humans, and then reinforcement learning, based on self-play. Finally, these two networks were embedded in a sophisticated search technique, called the *Monte Carlo tree search.*

Before the system was announced, DeepMind hired Fan Hui, a European Go champion, to play against AlphaGo: the system beat him five games to zero. This was the first time a Go program had beaten a human champion player in a full game. Shortly after, DeepMind announced that AlphaGo was going to be pitted against Lee Sedol, a world champion Go player, in a five-match competition to be held in Seoul, Korea, in March 2016.

The science of AlphaGo is fascinating, and AI researchers—myself included—were intrigued to see what would happen. (For the record, my guess was that AlphaGo might win one or two matches at most but that Sedol would decisively win the competition overall.) What none of us expected was the completely unprecedented wave of publicity that surrounded the competition. The event made headlines across the world, and the story of the competition was even made into a feature film.[14]

In the event, AlphaGo beat Lee Sedol four games to one: Lee lost the first three, came back to win the fourth, but lost the fifth. By all accounts, Lee was stunned to lose the first game—he expected to win easily. More than one person joked at the time that AlphaGo deliberately lost the fourth match so that Lee wouldn't feel so bad.

At various points in the competition, human commentators remarked on what seemed to be strange moves made by AlphaGo. They were, apparently, "not the kind of moves that a human would make." Of course, when we try to analyze how AlphaGo played, we do so from a very human standpoint. We instinctively look for the kind of motives and strategies that *we* would use when we play the game: we anthropomorphize. Trying to understand AlphaGo in this way is pointless; AlphaGo is a program that was optimized to do one single thing—to play the game of Go. We want to attribute motives and reasoning and strategy to the program, but there are none of these: AlphaGo's extraordinary capability is captured in the weightings in its neural nets. These neural nets are nothing more than very long lists of numbers, and we have no way of extracting or rationalizing the expertise that they embody.

One might think that two landmark achievements were enough, but just eighteen months later, DeepMind were in the news again, this time with a generalization of AlphaGo called AlphaGo Zero. The extraordinary thing about AlphaGo Zero is that it learned how to play to a superhuman level without any human supervision at all: *it just played against itself*.[15] To be fair, it had to play itself a *lot*, but nevertheless, it was a striking result, and it was further generalized in another follow-up system called AlphaZero, which learned to play a range of other games, including chess. After just nine hours of self-play, AlphaZero was able to consistently beat or draw against Stockfish, one of the world's leading dedicated chess-playing programs. The exciting thing here was the *generality* of the approach: AlphaGo could only play Go, and for all its cleverness at this, it had required considerable effort to build the system specifically for that. AlphaZero, it seemed, could be turned to many different types of board games.

Of course, we need to be careful not to read too much into these results. For one thing, although AlphaZero embodies an impressive degree of generality (it is a far more general expert game-playing program than any other program before it), it does not in itself represent a major advance toward general intelligence. It doesn't even remotely have the same kind of generality of intelligent capabilities that we all have. It can play board games superbly, but it can't converse or make a joke or cook an omelet or ride a bicycle or tie a pair of shoelaces. Its remarkable abilities are still actually very narrow. And of course, board games are highly abstract—they are a long way from the real world, as Rodney Brooks would be quick to remind us.

## TOWARD GENERAL AI?

Deep learning has proved to be enormously successful, in the sense that it has enabled us to build programs that we could not have imagined a few years ago. But laudable as these achievements genuinely are, they are not a magic ingredient that will propel AI toward the grand dream. Let me try to explain why. To do this, we'll look at two widely used applications of deep learning techniques: image captioning and automated translation.

In an image-captioning problem, we want a computer to be able to take an image and give a textual description of it. Systems that have this capability to some degree are now in widespread usage—the last update of my Apple Mac software gave me a photo management application that does a decent job of being able to classify my pictures into categories like "Beach scene," "Party," and so on. At the time of writing, several websites are available, typically run by international research groups, which allow you to upload photos and will attempt to provide captions for them. To better understand the limitations of current image captioning technology—and hence deep learning—I uploaded a family picture to one (in this case, Microsoft's CaptionBot)[16]— the photo is shown in figure 13.

Figure 13: What is going on in this picture?

Before examining CaptionBot's response, pause for a moment to look at the picture. If you are British or a fan of science fiction, then you will very probably recognize the gentleman on the right of the picture: he is Matt Smith, the actor who played the eponymous Doctor Who from 2010 to 2013 in the BBC television show. (You won't recognize the gentleman on the left—he is my late grandfather-in-law.)

CaptionBot's interpretation of the picture was as follows:

> I think it's Matt Smith standing posing for a picture and
> they seem :-) :-)

CaptionBot correctly identified a key element of the picture and went some way to recognizing the setting (standing; posing for a picture; smiling). However, this success can easily mislead us into thinking that CaptionBot is doing something that it most certainly is not—and what it is not doing is *understanding*. To illustrate this point, think about what it means for the system to identify Matt Smith. As we saw previously, machine learning systems like CaptionBot are trained by giving them a very large number of training examples, each example consisting of a picture together with a textual explanation of the picture. Eventually, after being shown enough pictures containing Matt Smith, together with the explanatory text "Matt Smith," the system is able to correctly produce the text "Matt Smith" whenever it is presented with a picture of the man himself.

But CaptionBot is not "recognizing" Matt Smith in any meaningful sense. To understand this, suppose I asked *you* to interpret what you see in the picture. You might come back with an explanation like this:

> I can see Matt Smith, the actor who played Doctor
> Who, standing with his arm around an older man—I
> don't know who he is. They are both smiling. Matt is
> dressed as his *Doctor Who* character, so he is probably
> filming somewhere. In his pocket is a rolled-up piece
> of paper, so that is likely to be a script. He is holding
> a paper cup, so he is probably on a tea break. Behind
> them, the blue box is the TARDIS, the spaceship / time

machine that Doctor Who travels around in. They are outdoors, so Matt is probably filming on location somewhere. There must be a film crew, cameras, and lights somewhere close by.

CaptionBot wasn't able to do any of that. While it was able to identify Matt Smith, in the sense of correctly producing the text "Matt Smith," it wasn't able to *use* this to then interpret and understand what is going on in the picture. And the absence of understanding is precisely the point here.

Apart from the fact that systems like CaptionBot only have a limited ability to interpret the pictures they are shown, there is another sense in which they do not, and currently cannot, demonstrate understanding of the kind that we can.

When you looked at the picture of Matt Smith dressed as Doctor Who, you would probably have experienced a range of thoughts and emotions, above and beyond simply identifying the actor and interpreting what was going on. If you were a Doctor Who fan, you might have found yourself reminiscing fondly about your favorite episode of *Doctor Who* with Matt Smith in the title role ("The Girl Who Waited," I hope we can all agree). You might have remembered watching Matt Smith as Doctor Who with your parents or your children. You might have remembered being scared by the monsters in the program, and so on. It might remind you of an occasion where you were on a film set or saw a film crew.

Your *understanding* of the picture is therefore grounded in your *experiences* as a person in the world. Such an understanding is not possible for CaptionBot, because CaptionBot has no such grounding (nor, of course, does it purport to). CaptionBot is completely *disembodied* from the world, and as Rodney Brooks reminded us, intelligence is *embodied*. I emphasize that this is not an argument that AI systems cannot demonstrate understanding but rather that understanding means more than being able to map a certain input (a picture containing Matt Smith) to a certain output (the text "Matt Smith"). Such a capability may be *part* of understanding, but it isn't by any means the whole story.

Automated translation from one language to another is another area in which deep learning has led to rapid progress over the past decade. Looking at what these tools can and cannot do helps us to understand the limitations of deep learning. Google Translate is probably the best-known automated translation system.[17] Originally made available as a product in 2006, the most recent versions of Google Translate use deep learning and neural nets. The system is trained by giving it large volumes of translated texts.

Let's see what happens when the 2019 iteration of Google Translate is given an unreasonably difficult problem: translating the first paragraph of *À la recherche du temps perdu* (*In Search of Lost Time*), the classic early-twentieth-century novel by the French author Marcel Proust. Here is the first paragraph, in the original French:

> *Longtemps, je me suis couché de bonne heure. Parfois, à peine ma bougie éteinte, mes yeux se fermaient si vite que je n'avais pas le temps de me dire: "Je m'endors." Et, une demi-heure après, la pensée qu'il était temps de chercher le sommeil m'éveillait; je voulais poser le volume que je croyais avoir encore dans les mains et souffler ma lumière; je n'avais pas cessé en dormant de faire des réflexions sur ce que je venais de lire, mais ces réflexions avaient pris un tour un peu particulier; il me semblait que j'étais moi-même ce dont parlait l'ouvrage: une église, un quatuor, la rivalité de François Ier et de Charles Quint.*

I'm embarrassed to say that, despite the decade-long efforts of a hardworking group of language teachers, I understand very little French: I can make out only the odd isolated phrase in the above text, and without help, I have no sense whatsoever of what the entire text means.

Here is that first paragraph, translated into English by a professional translator:[18]

> For a long time I used to go to bed early. Sometimes, when I had put out my candle, my eyes would close so quickly that I had not even time to say "I'm going to sleep." And half an hour later the thought that it was time to go to sleep would awaken me; I would try to put away the book which, I imagined, was still in my hands, and to blow out the light; I had been thinking all the time, while I was asleep, of what I had just been reading, but my thoughts had run into a channel of their own, until I myself seemed actually to have become the subject of my book: a church, a quartet, the rivalry between François I and Charles V.

Much better! But interestingly, although this is beautifully written English, the *meaning* is still not completely transparent, not to me, at least. What does the author mean when he writes, "I . . . seemed actually to have become the subject of my book: a church, a quartet, the rivalry between François I and Charles V"? How can you "become" a church? What does he mean by a "quartet"? What "rivalry" between François I and Charles V is he referring to? And for someone that uses electric lighting: What does it mean to "blow out" a light?

Now let's see what Google Translate made of it:

> Long time, I went to bed early. Sometimes, when my candle, my eyes would close so quickly that I had no time to say: "I fall asleep." And half an hour later the thought that it was time to go to sleep would awaken

> me; I wanted to ask the volume that I thought I had
> in my hands and blow my light; I had not ceased while
> sleeping to reflections on what I had read, but these
> reflections had taken a rather peculiar turn; I felt that I
> myself was what spoke the book: a church, a quartet, the
> rivalry between Francis I and Charles V.

This is recognizably the same text as the professional translation, and so Google Translate is doing something sophisticated. But you don't have to be a professional translator, or an expert on literature, to see its limitations. The expression "blow my light" makes no sense in English, and the sentences that follow don't make sense either. Indeed, they are rather comical. And the translation includes phrasings that a native English speaker would never use. The overall impression that we are getting is of a recognizable but unnaturally distorted version of the text.

Of course, we gave Google Translate an unreasonably difficult problem—translating Proust would be a huge challenge even for a professional French-to-English translator. So why is this, and why is it so hard for automated translation tools to tackle?

The point is that a translator of Proust's classic novel requires *more than just an understanding of French*. You could be the most competent reader of French in the world and still find yourself bewildered by Proust, and not just because of his frankly exhausting prose style. To properly *understand* Proust—and hence to properly *translate* Proust—you also need to have a great deal of background knowledge. Knowledge about French society and life in the early twentieth century (for example, you would need to know they used candles for lighting); knowledge of French history (of François I and Charles V and the rivalry between them); knowledge about early-twentieth-century French literature (the writing style of the time, allusions that authors might make); and knowledge about Proust himself (what were his main concerns?). A neural net of the type used in Google Translate has none of that.

This observation—that to *understand* Proust's text requires *knowledge* of various kinds—is not a new one. We came across it before, in the context of the Cyc project. Remember that Cyc was supposed to be given knowledge corresponding to the whole of consensus reality, and the Cyc hypothesis was that this would yield human-level general intelligence. Researchers in knowledge-based AI would be keen for me to point out to you that, decades ago, they anticipated exactly this issue. (The sharp retort from the neural nets community would then be that the techniques proposed by the knowledge-based AI community didn't work out so well, did they?) But it is not obvious that just continuing to refine deep learning techniques will address this problem. Deep learning will be part of the solution, but a proper solution will, I think, require something much more than just a larger neural net, or more processing power, or more training data in the form of boring French novels. It will require break-throughs at least as dramatic as deep learning itself. I suspect those breakthroughs will require explicitly represented knowl-edge as well as deep learning: somehow, we will have to bridge the gap between the world of explicitly represented knowledge, and the world of deep learning and neural nets.

## THE GREAT SCHISM

In 2010, I was asked to organize one of the big international AI meetings—the European Conference on AI (ECAI), which was to be held in Lisbon, Portugal. Attending conferences like ECAI are an important part of the life of an AI researcher. We write up our research results and submit them to the conference, where they are reviewed by a "program committee"—a group of eminent scientists who decide which of the submissions deserve to be heard at the conference. Good conferences in AI only accept about one in five submissions, so having a paper accepted is very prestigious; the really big AI conferences attract more than five thousand submissions. So you can imagine I felt very honored to be asked to chair the ECAI—it's an indication that the scientific community trusts you, and it is the sort of distinction that academics mention when they apply for a pay raise.

My job as chair included assembling the program committee, and I was keen to include a good representation from the machine learning community. But something unexpected happened: it seemed that every machine learning researcher I invited said no. It isn't unusual to be politely rebuffed when you are trying to persuade people into a role like this—after all, it is a lot of work. But it seemed I couldn't get *anyone* from machine learning to sign up. Was it me, I wondered? Or ECAI? Or what?

I sought advice from colleagues who had organized the event previously and others who had experience of other AI events. They reported similar experiences. The machine learning community, it seemed, just wasn't very interested in the events that I thought of as, well, "mainstream AI." I knew that the two big scientific events for the machine learning community were the Neural Information Processing Systems (NeurIPS) Conference and the International Conference on Machine Learning (ICML). Most subfields of AI have their own specialist conferences, so the fact that this community's attention should be focused on those was not surprising. But until then, it hadn't quite dawned on me that many in the machine learning community simply don't define themselves as being part of "AI" at all.

With hindsight, the schism between AI and ML seems to have started very early on: perhaps with the publication by Minsky and Papert of their 1969 book, *Perceptrons*, which, as we saw earlier, seems to have played a role in killing off neural AI research from the late 1960s until PDP emerged in the mid-1980s. Even in the present day, more than half a century later, there is still bitterness about the consequences of that publication. Whatever the origins of the schism, the truth is that, at some point, many in the machine learning research area diverged from mainstream AI and took off on their own trajectory. While there are certainly many researchers who see themselves as comfortably straddling the fence between machine learning and artificial intelligence, many machine learning experts nowadays would be surprised and possibly irritated to have the label "AI" attached to their work: because, for them, AI is the long list of failed ideas that I have documented elsewhere in this book.

# 6

## AI Today

DEEP LEARNING OPENED the floodgates for applications of AI. In the second decade of the twenty-first century, AI has attracted more interest than any new technology since the World Wide Web in the 1990s. Everyone with data and a problem to solve started to ask whether deep learning might help them—and in many cases, the answer proved to be *yes*. AI has started to make its presence felt in every aspect of our lives. Everywhere that technology is used, AI is finding applications: in education, science, industry, commerce, agriculture, health care, entertainment, the media and arts, and beyond. While some applications of AI will be very visible in the future, others will not. AI systems will be embedded throughout our world, in the same way that computers are today. And in the same way that computers and the World Wide Web changed our world, so too will AI. I could no more tell you what the full range of applications of AI will be than I could tell you about all the applications of computers, but here are a few of my favorite examples that have emerged during the past few years.

In April 2019, you may recall seeing the first ever pictures of a black hole.[1] In a mind-boggling experiment, astronomers used data collected from eight radio telescopes across the world to construct an image of a black hole that is forty billion miles across and fifty-five million light-years away. The image represents one of the most dramatic scientific achievements this century. But what you might *not* know is that it was only made possible through AI: advanced computer vision algorithms were used to reconstruct the image, "predicting" missing elements of the picture.

In 2018, researchers from the computer processor company Nvidia demonstrated the ability of AI software to create completely convincing but completely fake pictures of people.[2] The pictures were developed by a new type of neural network, one called a **generative adversarial network**. The pictures are uncanny: at first sight, they look utterly realistic, and it is hard to believe that they are not real people. The evidence of our eyes tells us that they are—but they were created by a neural net. This capability, unimaginable at the turn of the century, will be a key component of virtual reality tools in the future: AI is on the way to constructing convincing alternative realities.

In late 2018, DeepMind researchers at a conference in Mexico announced AlphaFold, a system to understand a fundamental issue in medicine called *protein folding*.[3] Protein folding involves predicting the shape that certain molecules will take on. Understanding the shapes that they will form is essential for progress in treating conditions such as Alzheimer's disease. Unfortunately, the problem is fearsomely difficult. AlphaFold used classic machine learning techniques to learn how to predict protein shapes and represents a promising step on the road to understanding these kinds of devastating conditions.

In the remainder of this chapter, I want to look in more detail at two of the most prominent opportunities for AI: the first is the use of AI in health care; the second is the long-held dream of driverless cars.

## AI-POWERED HEALTH CARE

Anybody with even the vaguest interest in politics and economics will recognize that the provision of health care is one of the most important global financial problems for private citizens and for governments. On the one hand, improvements in health care provision over the past two centuries are probably the most important single achievement of the scientific method in the industrialized world: in 1800, life expectancy for someone in Europe would have been less than fifty years;[4] someone born in Europe today could reasonably expect to live late into their seventies. Of course, these improvements in health care and life expectancy have not yet found their way to all the parts of the globe, but overall, the trend is positive, and this is, of course, a cause for celebration.

But these welcome advances have created challenges. First, populations are, on average, becoming older. And older people typically require more health care than younger people, which means that the overall cost of health care has risen. Second, as we develop new drugs and treatments for diseases and other afflictions, the overall range of conditions that we can treat increases—which also leads to additional health care costs. And of course, a key underlying reason for the expense of health care is that the resources required to deliver health care are expensive, and people with the skill and qualifications to do so are scarce.

Because of these problems, health care—and more particularly *funding* for health care—is everywhere a perennial issue for politicians to wrangle with. Wouldn't it be wonderful, then, if there was a *technological* fix to the health care problem?

The idea of AI for health care is nothing new—we saw earlier that the seminal MYCIN expert system was widely acclaimed after demonstrating better-than-human performance when diagnosing the causes of blood diseases in humans. No surprise, then, that MYCIN was followed by a wave of similar health care–related expert systems, although it is fair to say that relatively few of these made it far from their research labs. But nowadays, interest in AI for health care is back with a vengeance, and this time, there are several developments that suggest it has a better chance of succeeding on a large scale.

One important new opportunity for AI-powered health care is what we might call *personal health care management*. Personal health care management is made possible by the advent of *wearable technology*—smartwatches like the Apple Watch, and activity/fitness trackers such as Fitbit. These devices continually monitor features of our physiology such as our heart rate and body temperature. This combination of features raises the fascinating prospect of having large numbers of people generating data streams relating to their current state of health on a continual basis. These data streams can then be analyzed by AI systems, either locally (via the smartphone you carry in your pocket) or by uploading them to an AI system on the internet.

It is important not to underestimate the potential of this technology. For the first time ever, we can monitor our state of health on a continual basis. At the most basic level, our AI-based health care systems can then provide impartial advice on managing our health. This is, in some sense, what devices like Fitbit already do—they monitor our activity and can also set us targets.

Mass-market wearables are in their infancy, but there are plenty of indications of what is to come. In September 2018, Apple introduced the fourth generation of its Apple Watch, which included a heart monitor for the first time. Electrocardiogram apps on the phone can monitor the data provided by the heart-rate tracker and have the potential to identify the symptoms of heart diseases, perhaps even calling for an ambulance on your behalf if necessary. One possibility is monitoring for the elusive signs of atrial fibrillation—an irregular heartbeat—which can be the precursor to a stroke or other circulatory emergency. An accelerometer in the phone can be used to identify the signature of someone falling, potentially calling for assistance if needed. Such systems require only fairly simple AI techniques: what makes them practicable now is the fact that we can carry a powerful computer with us, which is continually connected to the internet, and which can be linked to a wearable device equipped with a range of physiological sensors.

Some applications of personal health care may not even require sensors, just a standard smartphone. Colleagues of mine at the University of Oxford believe it may be possible to detect the onset of dementia *simply from the way that someone uses their smartphone*. Changes in the way that people use their phone or changes in patterns of behavior recorded by their phone can indicate the onset of the disease, before any other person notices these signs and long before a formal diagnosis would normally be made. Dementia is a devastating condition and presents an enormous challenge for societies with aging populations. Tools that can assist with its early diagnosis or management would be very welcome. Such work is still at the very preliminary stages, but it provides yet another indicator of what might come.

This is all very exciting, but the opportunities presented by these new technologies come with some potential pitfalls too. The most obvious of these is privacy. Wearable technology is *intimate*: it continually watches us, and while the data it obtains can be used to help us, it also presents boundless opportunities for misuse.

One area of immediate concern is the insurance industry.

In 2016, the health insurance company Vitality started offering Apple Watches along with their insurance policies. The watches monitor your activity, and your insurance premiums are then set according to how much exercise you undertake. If, one month, you decided to be a couch potato and undertook no exercise, you might pay a full premium; but you could offset this the next month by going on a fitness frenzy, leading to a reduced premium. Perhaps there is nothing directly wrong with such a scheme, but it suggests some much more uncomfortable scenarios. For example, in September 2018, the U.S.-based insurance company John Hancock announced that in the future, it will *only* offer insurance policies to individuals who are prepared to wear activity-tracking technology.[5] The announcement was widely criticized.

Taking this kind of scenario further, what if we were only able to access national health care schemes (or other national benefits) if we agreed to be monitored and to meet daily exercise targets. You want health care? Then you have to walk ten thousand steps per day! Some people see nothing wrong with such a scenario; for others, it represents a profound intrusion and an abuse of our basic human rights.

Automated diagnosis is another exciting potential application for AI in health care. The use of machine learning to analyze data from medical imaging devices such as x-ray machines and ultrasound scanners has received enormous attention over the past decade. At the time of writing, it seems as if a new scientific article is announced showing that AI systems can effectively identify abnormalities from medical images every single day. This is a classic application of machine learning: we train the machine learning program by showing it examples of normal images and examples of abnormal images. The program learns to identify images with abnormalities.

A well-publicized example of this work came from DeepMind.

In 2018, the company announced they were working with Moorfields Eye Hospital in London to develop techniques to automatically identify diseases and abnormalities from eye scans.[6] Eye scans are a major activity for Moorfields: they typically undertake one thousand of them every working day, and analyzing these scans is a large part of the work of the hospital.

DeepMind's system used two neural networks, the first to "segment" the scan (identifying the different components of the image), and the second for diagnosis. The first network was trained on about nine hundred images, which showed how a human expert would segment the image; the second network was trained on about fifteen thousand examples. Experimental trials indicated that the system performed at or above the level of human experts.

You don't have to look far to find many other striking examples of how current AI techniques are being used to build systems with similar capabilities—for identifying cancerous tumors on x-rays, diagnosing heart disease from ultrasound scans, and many other examples.

Many have urged caution in the push for AI's use in health care. For one thing, the health care profession is, above all, a *human* profession: perhaps more than any other role, it requires the ability to interact with and relate to people. A GP needs to be able to "read" her patients, to understand the social context in which she is seeing them, to understand the kinds of treatment plans that are likely to work for this particular patient versus those which aren't, and so on. All the evidence indicates that we can now build systems that can achieve human expert performance in analyzing medical data—but this is only a small part (albeit a phenomenally important part) of what human health care professionals do.

Another argument against AI's use in health care is that some people would prefer to rely on human judgment rather than that of a machine. They would rather deal with a person. I think there are two points to make here.

First, it is hopelessly naive to hold up human judgment as some sort of gold standard. We are, all of us, flawed. Even the most experienced and diligent doctor will sometimes get tired and emotional. And however hard we try, we all fall prey to biases and prejudices, and often, we just aren't very good at rational decision-making. Machines *can* reliably make diagnoses that are every bit as good as those of human experts—the challenge/opportunity in health care is to put that capability to its best use. My belief is that AI is best used not to replace human health care professionals but to *augment* their capabilities—to free them from routine tasks and allow them to focus on the really difficult parts of their job; to allow them to focus on people rather than paperwork; and to provide another opinion— another voice in the room—to give further context for their work.

Second, the idea that we have a choice between dealing with a human physician or an AI health care program seems to me to be a first-world problem. For many people in other parts of the world, the choice may instead be between health care provided by an AI system or *nothing*. AI has a lot to offer here. It raises the possibility of getting health care expertise out to people in parts of the world who don't have access to it at present. Of all the opportunities that AI presents us with, it is this one that may have the greatest social impact.

## DRIVERLESS CARS

At the time of writing, more than a million people per year are dying in automobile-related accidents globally. A further fifty million people are injured every year in automobile accidents. These are staggering statistics, and yet we seem to be accustomed to the dangers of road travel—we accept the risk as an occupational hazard of living in the modern world. But AI holds out the real prospect of dramatically reducing those risks: driverless cars are a real possibility in the medium term, and ultimately, they have the potential to save lives on a massive scale.

There are, of course, many other good reasons for wanting autonomous vehicles. Computers can be programmed to drive cars *efficiently*, making better use of scarce and expensive fuel or power resources, resulting in environmentally friendlier cars with lower running costs. Computers could also potentially make better use of road networks, for example, allowing far greater throughput at congested road junctions. And if cars become safer, the need for them to have expensive and heavy protective chassis will be reduced, again leading to cheaper, more fuel-efficient vehicles. There is even an argument that driverless cars will make car ownership unnecessary: driverless taxis will be so cheap, goes the argument, that it won't make economic sense to own your own car.

For all these reasons and more, driverless cars are an obvious and compelling idea, and it will therefore be no surprise to you that there has been a long history of research in this area. As automobiles became mass-market products during the 1920s and 1930s, the scale of deaths and injuries that resulted—mostly because of human error—immediately prompted discussion about the possibility of automated cars. Although there have been a range of experiments in this field since the 1940s, it is only since the emergence of microprocessor technologies in the 1970s that they really began to be feasible. But the challenge of driverless cars is immense, and the fundamental problem is perception. If you could find a way for a car to know precisely where it was and what was around it, then you would have solved the problem of driverless cars. The solution to this problem was to be modern machine learning techniques: without them, driverless cars would not be possible.

The **PROMETHEUS** project, funded by the pan-governmental EUREKA organization in Europe, is widely seen as a forerunner of today's driverless car technology. PRO-METHEUS, which ran from 1987 to 1995, led to a demonstration in 1995, in which a car drove itself from Munich in Germany to Odense in Denmark and back. Human interventions were required on average about every five and a half miles; the longest stretch managed without human intervention was about a hundred miles. This was a remarkable feat—all the more remarkable because of the limited computer power available at the time. Although PROMETHEUS was only a proof that the concept could work and therefore a long way from a fully finished vehicle, the results of the project led to innovations that are now conventional in commercial automobiles, such as smart cruise control systems. And above all, PROMETHEUS signaled that this technology would, eventually, be commercially viable.

By 2004, progress was such that the U.S. military research agency DARPA organized a **Grand Challenge,** inviting researchers to enter a competition in which vehicles would autonomously traverse 150 miles of the American countryside. A total of 106 teams entered, from universities and companies alike, each hoping to win the $1 million prize offered by DARPA. These were whittled down to fifteen finalists, but in the event, none of the fifteen finalists completed more than eight miles of the course. Some vehicles failed to even make it out of the starting area. The most successful entry, Sandstorm from Carnegie Mellon University, managed just seven and a half miles, before going off course and getting stuck on an embankment.

My recollection of events at the time is that most AI researchers took the 2004 Grand Challenge as proof that driverless car technology was still some way from being practical. I was a little surprised to hear that DARPA had immediately announced a follow-up competition for 2005, with the prize money doubled to $2 million.

There were many more entries for the 2005 competition—195 in total, which were whittled down to 23 finalists. The final competition was held on October 8, 2005, and the goal was for the vehicles to cross 132 miles of the Nevada desert. This time, five teams completed the course. The winner was the robot **Stanley**, designed by a team from Stanford University, led by Sebastian Thrun. Stanley completed the course in just under seven hours, averaging about twenty miles per hour. A converted Volkswagen Touareg, Stanley was equipped with seven onboard computers, interpreting sensor data from GPS, laser range finders, radar, and video feed.

The 2005 Grand Challenge was one of the great technological achievements in human history. On that day, driverless cars became a solved problem, in the same way that heavier-than-air powered flight became a solved problem at Kitty Hawk just over a century earlier. The first flight by the Wright brothers lasted just twelve seconds, in which time the *Wright Flyer I* flew only 120 feet. But after that twelve-second journey, powered heavier-than-air flight was a reality—and so it was with driverless cars after the 2005 Grand Challenge.

The 2005 Grand Challenge was followed by a series of other challenges, of which probably the most important was the 2007 **Urban Challenge.** While the 2005 competition tested vehicles on rural roads, the 2007 challenge aimed to test them in built-up urban environments. Driverless cars were required to complete a course while obeying California road traffic laws and coping with everyday situations like parking, intersections, and traffic jams. Thirty-six teams made it to the national qualifying event, and of these eleven were selected for the final, held on a disused former airport on November 3, 2007. Six teams successfully completed the challenge, with the winner, from

Carnegie Mellon University, averaging approximately fourteen miles per hour throughout the four-hour challenge.

We have seen massive investment in driverless car technology since then, both from established automobile companies, who are desperate not to be left behind, and from newer companies, who perceive an opportunity to steal a march on traditional manufacturers.

In 2014, the U.S. Society of Automotive Engineers provided a useful classification scheme to characterize the various different levels of autonomy within a vehicle:[7]

> **Level 0: No autonomy:** The car has no automated control functions whatsoever. The driver is in complete control of the vehicle at all times (although the vehicle may provide warnings and other data to assist the driver). Level 0 includes the vast majority of cars on the roads today.

> **Level 1: Driver assistance:** Here the car provides some level of control for the driver, typically on routine matters, but the driver is expected to pay complete attention. An example of driver assistance would be an adaptive cruise control system, which can maintain the car's speed, using brakes and accelerator.

> **Level 2: Partial automation:** At this level, the car takes control of steering and speed, although again the driver is expected to be continually monitoring the driving environment and to be ready to intervene if necessary.

> **Level 3: Conditional automation:** At this level, the human driver is no longer expected to be continually monitoring the driving environment, although the car may ask the user to take control if it encounters a situation that it cannot cope with.

> **Level 4: High automation:** Here, the car takes control under normal circumstances, although the driver can still intervene.

> **Level 5: Full automation:** This is the dream of driverless cars: you get in a car, state your destination, and the car does everything from there. There is no steering wheel.

At the time of writing, the state-of-the-art system for commercially available driverless car technology is probably Tesla's Autopilot, initially available on the Tesla Model S car. Released in 2012, the Model S was the flagship vehicle in Tesla's lineup of high-specification electric cars, and at the time of its release, it was probably the world's most technologically advanced commercially available electric car. From September 2014 onward, all Tesla Model S vehicles were equipped with cameras, radar, and acoustic range sensors. The purpose of all this high-tech gear was made plain in October 2015, when Tesla released software for the car that enabled its Autopilot feature—a limited automatic driving capability.

The media was quick to start hailing Autopilot as the first driverless car, although Tesla was at pains to point out the limitations of the technology. In particular, Tesla insisted that drivers should keep their hands on the steering wheel at all times while Autopilot was engaged. In terms of the levels of autonomy presented above, Autopilot seemed to be at Level 2.

However good the technology was, it was obvious that serious accidents involving Autopilot would eventually occur and that the first fatality involving Autopilot would make headlines across the world. And this indeed proved to be the case when, in May 2016, a Tesla owner in Florida was killed when his car drove into an eighteen-wheel truck. Reports suggested that the car's sensors had been confused by the view of the white truck against a bright sky: as a consequence, the car's AI software failed to recognize there was another vehicle present and drove directly into the truck at high speed, instantly killing the driver.

Other incidents highlight what seems to be a key problem with current driverless car technology. At Level 0 autonomy, it is completely clear what is expected of the driver: everything. And at Level 5 autonomy, it is similarly obvious: the driver is expected to do nothing. But between these two extremes, it is much less evident what drivers must expect to do, and the anecdotal evidence from the Florida incident and elsewhere is that drivers place far too much reliance on the technology—treating it as if it were Level 4 or 5, when in fact it is far below this. This mismatch between driver expectations and the reality of what the system can do seems to be driven at least in part by an overexcited press, who don't seem to be very good at understanding or communicating the subtleties of technological capability. (It probably doesn't help that Tesla named their system Autopilot.)

In March 2018, another high-profile accident involving driverless cars raised further doubts about the technology. On March 18, 2018, in Tempe, Arizona, a driverless car owned by Uber hit and killed a forty-nine-year old pedestrian, Elaine Herzberg, while in driverless mode. As is typically the way with accidents of this kind, there were a number of contributory causes. The car was traveling faster than the automatic emergency braking system could handle, so by the time the car recognized that emergency braking was required, it was too late to be able to do anything about it. Although the car's sensors recognized that there was an "obstacle" (the victim, Elaine Herzberg), which called for emergency braking, the software seems to have been designed to avoid doing this (suggesting some confusion, or at least, a rather strange set of priorities, in the mind of the programmers). But most important, the "safety driver" in the car, whose main purpose was to intervene in incidents like this, appears to have been watching TV on her smartphone, paying little attention to the outside environment. It may well be that she was too confident in the car's driverless abilities as well. The tragic death of Elaine Herzberg was entirely avoidable—but the failure was human, not technological.

It seems depressingly inevitable that there will be more tragedies like these before we see practical, mass-market driverless cars. We need to do everything we reasonably can to anticipate and avoid such tragedies. But they will occur in any case; and when they do, we need to learn the lessons from them. The development of technologies such as fly-by-wire aircraft suggests that, in the long run, we will have much safer vehicles as a consequence.

The current flurry of activity around driverless vehicles suggests that the technology is tantalizingly close—but just *how* close is it? When will you be able to jump into a driverless car and state your destination? One of the most impartial indicators about this comes from information that driverless car companies are required to provide to the State of California in order to gain a license to test their cars within that state. The most important such piece of information is the Autonomous Vehicle Disengagement Report. The disengagement report must indicate how many miles the relevant car from which company drove in driverless mode and how many disengagements occurred during these tests. A disengagement is a situation in which a person had to intervene to take over control of the car—what *should* have occurred in the case of Elaine Herzberg. A disengagement doesn't necessarily mean that the person had to intervene to avoid an accident—far less a fatality—but nevertheless this data gives an indication of how well the technology is performing. The fewer disengagements per autonomous mile driven, the better.

In 2017, twenty companies filed disengagement reports with the State of California. The clear leader, in terms of number of miles driven and lowest number of disengagements per 1,000 miles, was a company called Waymo, who reported, on average, a disengagement about every 5,000 miles; the worst performance was by automobile giant Mercedes, who reported no fewer than 774 disengagements per 1,000 miles. Waymo is Google's driverless car company. Originally, it was an internal Google project, run by 2005 DARPA Grand Challenge winner

Sebastian Thrun, and it became part of a subsidiary company of Google in 2016. In 2018, Waymo reported traveling 11,000 miles between disengagements.

So what does this data tell us? And in particular, how soon will driverless cars be an everyday reality?

Well, the first conclusion we can draw, from the relatively poor performance of automobile giants like BMW, Mercedes, and Volkswagen, is that a historical track record in the automotive industry is *not* the key requirement for success in driverless car technology. On reflection, this should come as no surprise: the key to driverless cars is not the internal combustion engine but *software*—AI software. No surprise, then, that the U.S. automobile giant General Motors acquired driverless car company Cruise Automation for an undisclosed (but obviously very large) sum in 2016, while Ford invested $1 billion in self-driving start-up company Argo AI. Both companies made public, very ambitious claims about the rollout of commercial driverless cars: Ford predicted they would have a "fully autonomous vehicle in commercial operation" by 2021.[8]

Of course, we don't know the precise criteria that companies use to decide when a disengagement occurs. It could be that Mercedes, for example, are just being overly cautious. But it seems hard to avoid the conclusion that, at the time of writing, Waymo are far ahead of the pack.

It is interesting to compare the State of California disengagement reports with what we know about human-driver performance. There doesn't seem to be any definitive statistical data about the latter, but it seems that in the United States, humans drive on average hundreds of thousands of miles between serious incidents—possibly even a million. This suggests that even the market leader, Waymo, would have to improve their technology by up to two orders of magnitude before they can achieve a comparable level of safety on the road to that of human drivers. Of course, not all the disengagements reported by Waymo would have led to accidents, so the comparison is hardly scientific, but at least it gives some indication of the scale of the challenges still faced by driverless car companies.

Anecdotally, speaking to engineers who work with driverless cars, it seems the key difficulty for the technology is dealing with unexpected events. We can train cars to deal with *most* eventualities—but what happens when the car meets a situation that is unlike anything it has met in training? While most driving scenarios are routine and expected, there is a long tail of completely unpredictable situations that could occur. In such a situation, a human driver would have their own experience of the world to fall back on. They could think about how to handle it, and if they don't have time to think, they can call upon their instincts. Driverless cars do not have this luxury— and won't, not for the foreseeable future.

Another major challenge is how to make the transition from the current state of affairs on our roads (all vehicles on the roads are driven by people) through a mixed scenario (some human-driven cars, some driverless) to a completely driverless future. On the one hand, autonomous vehicles just don't behave like people while driving, and this confuses and unnerves the human drivers they share the roads with. On the other hand, human drivers are unpredictable and don't necessarily follow the rules of the road to the letter, making it hard for AI software to understand their behavior and interact with them safely.

Given my upbeat assessment of the progress made in driverless car technology, this may sound surprisingly pessimistic. So let me do my best to explain how I think events might unfold in the decades ahead.

First, I believe driverless car technology *in some form* will be in everyday use soon—likely within the next decade. However, this doesn't mean that Level 5 autonomy is imminent. Instead,

I think we will start to see the technology rolled out in specific "safe" niche areas and that it will gradually then start to make its way out into the wider world.

So in what niches do I think we will see the technology in widespread use? Mining is one example. Perhaps in the giant open-cast mines of Western Australia or Alberta, Canada: there are comparatively few people there—far fewer pedestrians and cyclists behaving erratically. In fact, the mining industry already uses autonomous vehicle technology on a large scale. For example, the British-Australian Rio Tinto mining group claimed in 2018 that more than a billion tons of ore and minerals had been transported by their fleet of giant autonomous trucks in the Pilbara region of Western Australia,[9] although from the publicly available information, it seems the trucks are quite some way from Level 5 autonomy—more "automated" than "autonomous." Nevertheless, this seems like a good example of driverless vehicles being used to great effect in a constrained environment.

In much the same way, factories, ports, and military installations all seem well suited to driverless vehicles. I feel confident that we will see large-scale take-up of driverless technology in these areas within the next few years.

For driverless technology in everyday use beyond these niche applications, there are several possible scenarios, some or all of which may come to pass. It seems quite likely that we will see low-speed "taxi pods" in well-mapped, constrained urban environments or on specified routes. Indeed, several companies are trialing similar services at the time of writing, albeit on a very limited basis (and for the time being, with human "safety drivers" present in cars to handle emergencies). Limiting such vehicles to low speeds is hardly likely to be seen as a problem in cities like London, where traffic moves very slowly in any case.

Another possibility is special driverless car lanes in cities and on major highways. Most cities already have bus lanes and cycle lanes, so why not driverless car lanes? Such lanes might be augmented by sensors and other technology to assist autonomous vehicles. The presence of such lanes would also send a clear signal to human drivers sharing the roads with autonomous vehicles: beware robot drivers!

As to the question of Level 5 autonomy, we are still some distance away, I'm afraid. But it is inevitable. My best guess is that it will be at least twenty years from the time of writing before Level 5 autonomous vehicles are widely available. But I am pretty confident that my grandchildren will regard the idea that their grandfather actually drove a car *on his own* with a mixture of horror and amusement.

# 7

## How We Imagine Things Might Go Wrong

THE RAPID PROGRESS we've witnessed in AI since the turn of the century has led to a lot of press coverage. Some of this coverage is balanced and reasonable; much of it is frankly rather silly. Some of it is informative and constructive; much of it is nothing more than scaremongering. In July 2017, for example, it was widely reported that Facebook had closed down two AI systems after they had begun to converse in their own made-up language (which was apparently incomprehensible to their designers).[1] The clear implication in headlines and social media postings at the time was that Facebook shut down the systems because they were afraid they were losing control. In fact, the Facebook experiment was completely routine and totally harmless. It was the kind of experiment that a student might undertake as a project. There was no more possibility of the Facebook systems running amok than there is of your toaster transforming itself into a killer robot. It was, simply, impossible.

While on the one hand I found coverage of the Facebook incident rather comical, it also left me deeply frustrated. The problem is, reporting of this kind panders to the *Terminator* narrative of AI: that we are creating something we won't be able to control, which could pose an existential risk to humanity (you can almost hear a voice-over from Arnold Schwarzenegger in his classic role).

This narrative still dominates the debate about the future of AI, which is now routinely discussed in tones previously reserved for nuclear weapons. Elon Musk, the billionaire entrepreneur and cofounder of PayPal and Tesla, was sufficiently worried by this idea that he made a series of public statements expressing his concerns and donated $10 million in research funding to support responsible AI; in 2014, Stephen Hawking, then the world's most famous scientist, publicly stated that he feared AI represented an existential threat to humanity.

The *Terminator* narrative is damaging, for several reasons. First, it makes us worry about things that we probably don't need to fret about. But second, it draws attention away from those issues raised by AI that we *should* be concerned about. These may not make good headlines like *The Terminator*, but they are probably the issues that we should be concerned about *now*. So in this chapter, I want to address the headline fears about AI: the possibility of *Terminator* scenarios and how AI might go wrong. I will start, in the next section, by tackling this narrative head-on. We'll discuss how it might happen and how likely it is. This then leads us to a discussion of ethical AI—the possibility of AI systems acting as moral agents and the various frameworks for ethical AI that have been proposed. I'll conclude by drawing attention to one particular feature of AI systems in which they *are* prone to failure, albeit not at a highly scary level: if we want an AI system to act on our behalf, then we need to communicate to it what we want. But this turns out to be hard to do, and if we don't take care when communicating our desires, then we may get what we asked for, but not what we actually *wanted*.

## TERMINATING THE TERMINATOR

In contemporary AI, the *Terminator* narrative is most commonly associated with an idea called the **singularity,** which was introduced by the American futurologist Ray Kurzweil in his 2005 book, *The Singularity Is Near.*[2]

> The key idea underlying the impending Singularity is that the pace of change of our human-created technology is accelerating and its powers are expanding at an exponential pace. . . . within several decades information-based technologies will encompass all human knowledge and proficiency, ultimately including the pattern-recognition powers, problem-solving skills, and emotional and moral intelligence of the human brain itself.

Although Kurzweil's vision of the singularity is quite broad, the term has come to be identified with one specific idea: the singularity is the hypothesized point at which computer intelligence (in the general sense) exceeds that of humans. At this point, it is suggested, computers could start to apply their own intelligence to improving themselves, and this process will then start to feed off itself. After that, these improved machines will then apply their improved intelligence to improving themselves further, and so on. From that point on, so the argument goes, it will be impossible for mere human intelligence to regain control.

It's a very compelling idea—and a deeply alarming one. But let's pause for a moment to examine the logic behind the singularity. In a nutshell, Kurzweil's main argument hinges on the idea that computer hardware (processors and memory) is developing at such a rate that the information-processing capacity of computers will soon exceed that of the human brain. His argument derives from a well-known dictum in computing called Moore's law, named after Gordon Moore, a cofounder of

Intel, who formulated it in the mid-1960s. Moore's law states that the number of transistors that can fit on a fixed area of a semiconductor doubles about every eighteen months. The practical upshot of Moore's law is that, to put it crudely, computer processors can be expected to roughly double in power every eighteen months. Moore's law has several important corollaries, among them that computer-processing power could be expected to get progressively cheaper at the same rate and that processors themselves to get progressively smaller. Moore's law proved very reliable for nearly fifty years, although some current processor technologies started to hit the physical limits of their capabilities around 2010.

Now, Kurzweil's argument implicitly links the inevitability of the singularity to the availability of raw computer power implied by Moore's law. But this link is dubious. Indulge me, for a moment, with a thought experiment. Imagine that we could download your brain into a computer (we are in the realm of pure fantasy here, of course), and suppose the computer we download your brain into is the fastest, most powerful computer ever. With all this amazing processing power at your command, would you be superintelligent? For sure, you'd be able to "think quickly"—but does that make you more *intelligent*? In some trivial sense, I guess it does—but not in any meaningful sense of intelligence and not in the sense of the singularity.[3] Raw computer-processing power, in other words, will not inevitably lead to the singularity. It is probably a *necessary* requirement for it (we won't achieve human-level intelligence without highly powered computers), but it isn't a *sufficient* requirement (simply having highly powered computers won't get us to human-level intelligence). To put it another way, AI software (machine learning programs, for example) improves at a much, much slower pace than the hardware.

There are other reasons to doubt whether the singularity is

in prospect.[4] For one thing, even if AI systems did become as intelligent as people, it does not follow that they would be able to improve themselves at some rate beyond our ability to understand. As this book has shown, *we* have made only rather slow progress on AI over the past sixty years—what evidence is there that human-level general AI will be able to make AI progress faster?

A related argument concerns the idea of AI systems working with each other together to achieve intelligence beyond our ability to comprehend or control it (cf. the Facebook incident I mentioned at the start of the chapter). But I don't find this argument very convincing either. Suppose you got together a thousand clones of Einstein. Would their collective intelligence be a thousand times that of Einstein? In fact, I suspect their collective intelligence would be considerably less than that. Again, although our thousand Einsteins would be able to collectively do some things *faster* than one Einstein could, that isn't the same as being *smarter*.

For these reasons and more, many AI researchers are skeptical about the singularity, at least for the foreseeable future. We know of no path that will take us from where we are now, in terms of computing and AI technology, to the singularity. But some serious commentators are still worried and claim these arguments are complacency. They point to the experience of nuclear energy. Back in the early 1930s, scientists knew that there was a huge amount of energy locked in the nuclei of atoms, but had no idea how to release it or even if that was possible. Some scientists were extremely dismissive of the idea that nuclear energy could be harnessed: Lord Rutherford, one of the most famous scientists of his age, said it was "moonshine" to imagine that we would be able to tap into this energy source. But famously, the day after Rutherford dismissed the possibility of nuclear energy, the physicist Leo Szilard was crossing a road in London, mulling over Rutherford's pronouncement, when the idea of a nuclear chain reaction suddenly occurred to him. Just over a decade later, two Japanese cities were destroyed by bombs powered in the way that Szilard had imagined in a split second. Could there be a Leo Szilard moment in AI—a sudden insight that would quickly take us to the singularity? Of course, we can't rule it out, but it is highly unlikely. A nuclear chain reaction is actually a very simple mechanism—a high-school student can understand it. All the experience of AI research over the last sixty years tells us that human-level AI is not.

But what about the distant future—a hundred years ahead or a thousand? Here, I have to admit that things are much less clear. It would be unwise to try to predict what computer technology will be capable of in a hundred years, still less a thousand. But it seems highly unlikely to me that, if the singularity occurs, it will take us by surprise, as in the *Terminator* narrative. To use an analogy by Rodney Brooks, think of human-level intelligence as a Boeing 747. Is it likely that we would invent a Boeing 747 by accident? Or that we would develop a Boeing 747 without expecting to? A counterresponse is that, although it might be *unlikely*, the consequences for us all if it *did* occur would be so dramatic that this justifies thinking and planning ahead for the singularity now.

## WE NEED TO TALK ABOUT ASIMOV

Whenever I discuss the *Terminator* narrative with a lay audience, somebody suggests that what we need are something like the **Three Laws of Robotics,** formulated by the renowned science fiction author Isaac Asimov. The Three Laws were invented by Asimov in a series of stories about robots equipped with a version of strong AI via what he called *positronic brains*. Asimov first formulated the laws in 1939, and over the next four decades, they provided him with an ingenious plot device for what would ultimately become a celebrated series of short stories and a disappointing Hollywood movie.[5] The "science" of the AI in Asimov's stories—positronic brains—is meaningless, although of course the stories are nonetheless entertaining for that. What is interesting for our purposes are the laws themselves:

1. A robot may not injure a human or, through inaction, allow a human to come to harm.

2. A robot must obey orders given by humans except where they would conflict with the First Law.

3. A robot must protect its own existence as long as this does not conflict with the First or Second Laws.

The laws are beautifully formulated and at first sight appear to be ingeniously robust. Could we design AI systems with these laws built in?

Well, the first thing to say about Asimov's laws is that, ingenious though they are, many of Asimov's stories were based upon situations in which the laws turned out to be flawed or led to contradictions. In the story "Runaround," for example, a robot called SPD-13 seems destined to endlessly circle a pool of molten selenium because of a conflict between the need to obey an order (the Second Law) and the need to protect itself (the Third Law)—it orbits the pool at a fixed distance because, if it gets any closer, the need to protect itself kicks in, while if it gets any farther away, the need to obey kicks in. There are many other examples in his stories (and if you haven't done so already, I urge you to read them). So the laws themselves, ingenious as they are, certainly aren't by any means watertight.

But the bigger problem with Asimov's laws is that implementing them within an AI system just isn't feasible.

Think about what it would mean to implement the First Law, for example. Every time an AI system was contemplating an action, it would need to consider the effects that this action might have, presumably on *all* humans (or is it only some that matter?), and into the future too (or do you only care about the here and now?). This is not feasible. And the "or, through inaction" clause is equally problematic—should a system constantly contemplate *all* its possible actions with respect to *every* person to see whether the relevant action prevents harm? Again, it just won't work.

Even capturing the notion of "harm" is difficult. Consider: when you fly on a plane from London to Los Angeles, you are consuming a large amount of natural resources and generating a lot of pollution and carbon dioxide along the way. This is almost certainly harming someone but in such a way that it is impossible to precisely quantify it. A robot that obeyed Asimov's laws literally would not, I think, be persuaded onto an airplane or into an automobile. Actually, I doubt it would be able to do very much at all—it would likely be huddled in a corner somewhere, hiding from the world, crippled by indecision.

So if Asimov's laws—and other well-intentioned systems of ethical principles for AI—don't necessarily help us, how should we think about the acceptable behavior of AI systems?

## WE NEED TO STOP TALKING ABOUT THE TROLLEY PROBLEM

Asimov's laws can be seen as the first and most famous attempt to formulate an overarching framework to govern decision-making in AI systems. Although it wasn't intended as a serious ethical framework for AI, we can see it as the ancestor of a whole host of such frameworks that have appeared alongside the recent growth of AI and have been the subject of serious research.[6] In the remainder of this chapter, we will survey this work and discuss whether or not it is heading in the right direction. We'll begin our survey with one particular scenario that has attracted more attention in the ethical AI community than perhaps any other.

The **trolley problem** is a thought experiment in the philosophy of ethics, originally introduced by British philosopher Philippa Foot in the late 1960s.[7] Her aim in introducing the trolley problem was to disentangle some of the highly emotive issues surrounding the morality of abortion. There are many versions of Foot's trolley problem, but the most common version goes something like this (see figure 14):

A trolley (i.e., a tram) has gone out of control and is careering at high speed toward five people who are unable to move. There is a lever by the track; if you pull the lever, then the trolley will be diverted down an alternative track, where there is just one person (who also cannot move). If you pull the lever, then this person would be killed, but the five others would be saved.

Should you pull the lever or not?

**Figure 14:** The trolley problem. If you do nothing, the five people on the upper track will die; if you pull the lever, the person on the lower track will die. What should you do?

The trolley problem has risen rapidly in prominence recently because of the imminent arrival of driverless cars. Pundits were quick to point out that driverless cars might find themselves in a situation like the trolley problem, and AI software would then be called upon to make an impossible choice. "Self-Driving Cars Are Already Deciding Who to Kill" ran one internet headline in 2016.[8] There was a flurry of anguished online debate, and several philosophers of my acquaintance were surprised and flattered to discover that there was suddenly an attentive audience for their opinions on what had hitherto been a rather obscure problem in the philosophy of ethics.

Despite its apparent simplicity, the trolley problem raises some surprisingly complex issues. My intuitive response to the problem is, all other things being equal, I would pull the lever because it would be better to have just one person die rather than five. Philosophers call this kind of reasoning *consequentialist* (because it assesses the morality of actions on the basis of their consequences). The best-known consequentialist theory is **utilitarianism.** It has its origins in the work of eighteenth-century British philosopher Jeremy Bentham and his student John Stuart Mill. They formulated an idea called the *greatest happiness principle,* which, speaking approximately, says that one should choose whichever action maximizes the "aggregate happiness of the world." While the general principle seems appealing, making the idea of the "aggregate happiness of the world" precise is not easy. For example, suppose the five individuals in the trolley problem are evil mass murderers, while the other individual is an innocent young child. Do the lives of five evil mass murderers outweigh that of an innocent young child? If not five, suppose there were ten mass murderers—would that be enough for you to decide to pull the lever and save the killers at the expense of a child's life?

An alternative point of view is that an action is acceptable if it is consistent with some general "good" principle, the standard example being that taking life is wrong. If you adhere to the principle that taking life is wrong, then *any* action that causes a death would be unacceptable. Someone who accepted such a principle would not take action in response to the trolley problem, since their action would cause someone's death—even though *not* acting leads to five other deaths.

A third standpoint is based on the idea of **virtue ethics.** From this standpoint, we might identify a "virtuous person," who embodies the virtues that we aspire to in a decision-maker, and then say that the correct choice is the choice that would be made by this sort of person in this setting.

Of course, in AI, the decision-maker would be an agent—a driverless car, which must choose between driving straight ahead and killing five people or swerving and killing one. So what would and what should an AI agent do when faced with a trolley problem or something like it?

Well, first, we should ask ourselves whether it is reasonable to expect *more* of an AI system than we would expect of a person in a situation like this. If the greatest philosophical thinkers in the world cannot definitively resolve the trolley problem, then is it reasonable of us to expect an AI system to do so?

Second, I should point out that I have been driving cars for decades, and in all that time, I have never faced a trolley problem. Nor has anyone else I know. Moreover, what I know about ethics, and the ethics of the trolley problem, is roughly what you read earlier: I wasn't required to pass an ethics exam to get my driver's license. This has not been a problem for me so far. Driving a car does not require deep ethical reasoning—so requiring that driverless cars can resolve the trolley problem before we put them on the roads therefore seems to me a little absurd.

Third, the truth is that however obvious the answers to ethical problems might seem to *you,* other people will have *different* answers, which seem just as self-evident to them.

Intriguing and ingenious though it undoubtedly is, the trolley problem does not, I think, have much of value to tell us about AI software for driverless cars. I don't believe that the driverless cars we are likely to encounter in the coming decades will do ethical reasoning of this type. So what *would* a real driverless car do *in practice,* when faced with a situation like the trolley problem? The likeliest outcome would be that the car would just slam on the brakes. And perhaps, in practice, that is probably all that we would manage to do in the same situation.

## THE RISE OF ETHICAL AI

Of course, there are much wider issues around AI and ethics, which are perhaps of more immediate importance and relevance than the arguably rather artificial trolley problem, and at the time of writing, these issues are being keenly debated. Every technology company, it seems, wants to demonstrate that *their* AI is more ethical than everyone else's—scarcely a week goes by without a press release announcing a new ethical AI initiative. It is worth reflecting on these a little and the role they are likely to play in how AI develops in the years to come.

One of the first and most influential frameworks for ethical AI was the **Asilomar principles,** which were formulated by a group of AI scientists and commentators who met in the Californian resort of the same name in 2015 and 2017. The main deliverable was a set of twenty-three principles, which AI scientists and developers across the world were asked to ascribe to.[9] Most of the Asilomar principles are pretty uncontentious: the first is that the goal of AI research should be to create beneficial intelligence; the sixth is that AI systems should be safe and secure; and the twelfth is that people should have the right to access, manage, and control data that relates to them.

Some of the principles, however, seem rather aspirational: the fifteenth, for example, requires that "the economic prosperity created by AI should be shared broadly, to benefit all of humanity." I personally have no difficulty in ascribing to this principal, but I'm afraid I think it is naive to imagine that big business will do anything more than pay lip service to it. Big businesses are investing in AI because they hope it will give them a competitive advantage that will deliver benefits to their shareholders, not because they want to benefit humanity.[10]

The final five principles relate to the long-term future of AI:

- **Capability Caution:** There being no consensus, we should avoid strong assumptions regarding upper limits on future AI capabilities.

- **Importance:** Advanced AI could represent a profound change in the history of life on earth and should be planned for and managed with commensurate care and resources.

- **Risks:** Risks posed by AI systems, especially catastrophic or existential risks, must be subject to planning and mitigation efforts commensurate with their expected impact.

- **Recursive Self-Improvement:** AI systems designed to recursively self-improve (automatically improve their intelligence, and then use their improved intelligence to improve themselves further) or self-replicate in a manner that could lead to rapidly increasing quality or quantity must be subject to strict safety and control measures.

- **Common Good:** Superintelligence should only be developed in the service of widely shared ethical ideals and for the benefit of all humanity rather than one state or organization.

Again, I have no difficulty at all in ascribing to these principles, but we are so far from the scenarios hinted at here becoming a reality that including them almost amounts to scaremongering. Maybe these issues *will* be worth losing sleep over at some point in the future, but to give them prominence now presents a misleading picture of where AI is and, more worryingly, distracts us from the problems that we *should* be concerned about, which we will discuss in the next chapter. Of course, because the scenarios indicated here are likely to be a long way in the future, it doesn't cost companies anything to sign up to them, and it makes for good publicity.

In 2018, Google released their own guidelines for ethical AI. Somewhat pithier than the Asilomar principles, they cover much of the same territory (being beneficial, avoiding bias, being safe), and helpfully, Google also provided some concrete guidance around best practices in AI and machine learning development.[11] Another framework was proposed by the European Union at the end of 2018,[12] and yet another by the IEEE (a key professional organization for computing and IT);[13] many major companies—and not just IT companies—have also released ethical AI guidelines of their own.

It is, of course, wonderful that big businesses are declaring their commitment to ethical AI. The difficulty, though, is understanding precisely what they have committed to. High-level aspirations, such as sharing the benefits of AI, are welcome, but translating that into specific actions is not easy. The company motto used by Google for more than a decade was "Don't be evil." What precisely does that mean for Google's employees? They need much more specific guidance if they are to prevent Google from crossing over to the Dark Side.

Within the various frameworks that have been proposed, certain themes recur, and there is increasing consensus around these. My colleague Virginia Dignum at Umeå University in Sweden has championed these issues, and she distills them into three key concepts: accountability, responsibility, and transparency.[14]

Accountability in this sense means that, for example, if an AI system makes a decision that significantly affects someone, then they have a right to an explanation for that decision. But what counts as an explanation is a difficult issue, one which will have different answers in different settings, and current machine learning systems are not capable of providing explanations.

Responsibility means that it should always be clear who is responsible for a decision and, crucially, that we should not try to claim that an AI system was "responsible" for a decision: the responsible party will be individuals or organizations that deployed the system. This points toward a deeper philosophical issue, one relating to the question of **moral agency.**

A moral agent is commonly understood to be an entity that is capable of distinguishing right and wrong, and of understanding the consequences of their actions with respect to such distinctions. It is often imagined in popular discussion that AI systems are, or can be, moral agents and can be held accountable for their actions. The general view in the AI community is that this is not the case: software can't be held responsible. Rather, responsibility must lie with those that develop and deploy the technology.

More generally, responsibility in AI doesn't imply building machines that are themselves morally responsible but rather developing AI systems in a responsible way. For example, distributing a Siri-like software agent that misled users into believing that they were interacting with another person would be an irresponsible use of AI by the developers of it. The software isn't culpable here: those who develop and deploy it are. Responsible design here would mean that the AI would always make it clear that it is nonhuman.

Finally, transparency means that the data that a system uses about us should be available to us and the algorithms used within that should be made clear to us too.

## BE CAREFUL WHAT YOU WISH FOR

The discussion of ethical AI sometimes makes us forget one of the more mundane realities about how things might go wrong: AI software is, well, *software,* and we don't need any fancy new technologies for software to go wrong. The problem of developing bug-free software is a huge research area in computing—finding and eliminating bugs is one of the main activities in software development. But AI provides novel new ways for bugs to be introduced. One of the most important of these arises from the fact that, if AI software is to work on our behalf, then we need to tell it what we want it to do. And this is often not nearly as easy as it might appear.

About fifteen years ago, I was working on techniques intended to enable vehicles to coordinate themselves without human intervention. The particular scenario I was working on was a railway network. This makes it sound much more impressive than it actually was, because the "network" I was looking at consisted of two trains traveling in opposite directions on a circular railway. And they were virtual trains—no actual railway track was involved (not even a toy railway track, actually). At one point, the pretend railway passed through a narrow tunnel, and if ever both trains entered the tunnel at the same time, then there would be a (simulated) crash. My goal was to prevent this. I was trying to develop a general framework that would allow me to present a goal to my system (the goal in this case being to prevent a crash) so that the system would come back with some rules that, if the trains followed them, would be guaranteed to ensure that my goal was achieved (the trains wouldn't crash).

My system worked, but not in the way I had in mind. The first time I presented my goal, the system came back with the following recommendation: *Both trains must remain stationary.* Well, of course this works—if both trains remain stationary, then no crash will occur—but it wasn't the kind of solution I was after.

The problem I encountered is a standard one in AI and indeed in computer science generally. The problem is this: we want to *communicate our desires* to a computer so that the computer can pursue them on our behalf, but communicating our desires to a computer is a deeply problematic process, for several reasons.

First, we may ourselves not know what we actually want—at least not explicitly—and in this case, articulating our desires is going to be impossible. Often, our desires will be contradictory—in which case, how is an AI system to make sense of them?

Moreover, it may be impossible to spell out our preferences in toto, so the best we will often be able to do is give a snapshot of our preferences, leaving gaps in the overall picture. How, then, should the AI system fill in the gaps?

But finally, and perhaps most important, when we communicate with *people,* we usually assume that we share *common values and norms.* We don't explicitly spell these out every time we interact. But an AI system doesn't know about these values and norms. So they either have to be explicitly spelled out, or else we somehow have to make sure that the AI system has them in the background. If they aren't there, then we may not get what we really wanted. In the train scenario above, I communicated my goal that the trains were to avoid crashing but forgot to convey that they should still be allowed to move. I had forgotten that although a human would, almost certainly, implicitly understand that this was my intention, a computer system would not.

Scenarios like this were popularized by Oxford philosopher Nick Bostrom in his bestselling 2014 book *Superintelligence.*[15] He calls this **perverse instantiation:** the computer does what you asked for, but not in the way you anticipated. Hours of fun are to be had dreaming up other perverse instantiation scenarios: you ask a robot to prevent deaths from cancer, so it murders everyone, and so on.

Of course, this is a problem that we encounter repeatedly in everyday life: whenever someone designs a system of incentives that are intended to encourage a certain behavior, someone else will find a way to game the system, gaining the rewards without behaving as intended. I am reminded of a (possibly apocryphal) story from the era of Soviet Russia. The Russian government wanted to incentivize the production of cutlery and so decided to reward factories that produced cutlery according to the *weight* of cutlery they produced. What happened? Cutlery factories quickly started to produce *very* heavy cutlery . . .

Aficionados of classic Disney films may recognize a closely related type of problem. The 1940 Disney film *Fantasia* features a segment in which a naive young sorcerer's apprentice (Mickey Mouse) becomes tired of his chore of carrying water into the house from a well. To relieve himself of the burden, he brings a broomstick to life to do this for him. But Mickey dozes off, and upon waking up, his attempts to stop the broomstick bringing in water, bucket after bucket, result in ever more magical broomsticks flooding his basement. It requires the intervention of his master, the sorcerer, to rectify the problem. Mickey got what he asked for, but not what he wanted.

Bostrom also considered these types of scenarios. He imagined an AI system that controlled the manufacture of paper clips. The system is given the goal of maximizing the production of paper clips, which it takes literally, transforming first the earth and then the rest of the universe into paper clips. Again, the problem is ultimately one of communication: in this case, when we communicate our goal, we need to be sure that acceptable boundaries are understood.

The challenge in all these scenarios is for the computer to understand *what it is we really want*. The field of **inverse reinforcement learning** is directed at this problem. We saw regular reinforcement learning in chapter 5: an agent acts in some environment and receives a reward; the learning challenge is to find a course of actions that maximize the reward received. In inverse reinforcement learning, we instead get to see "ideal" behavior (what a *person* would do); the challenge is then to figure out what the relevant rewards are for the AI software.[16] In short, the idea is to look at human behavior as our model for desirable behavior.

# 8

## How Things Might Actually Go Wrong

ALTHOUGH I AM a skeptic with respect to the possibility of an imminent singularity, that doesn't mean that I believe we have nothing to fear from AI. After all, AI is a general-purpose technology: its applications are limited only by our imagination. All such technologies have unintended consequences, being felt decades or even centuries into the future, and all such technologies have the potential for abuse. Our anonymous prehistoric ancestors who first harnessed fire should surely be forgiven for not anticipating the climactic changes that would result from burning fossil fuels. British scientist Michael Faraday, inventing the electric generator in 1831, probably didn't anticipate the electric chair. Karl Benz, who patented the automobile in 1886, surely could not have foretold the million deaths a year that his invention would be causing a century in the future. And Vint Cerf, inventor of the internet, probably didn't imagine terrorist groups sharing beheading videos via his innocent creation.

Like all these technologies, AI will have adverse consequences that will be felt on a global scale, and like all these technologies, it will be abused. These consequences may not be quite as dramatic as the *Terminator* narrative that I sought to dispel in the previous chapter, but they are the ones that we and our descendants will need to grapple with in the decades to come.

In this chapter, therefore, I will discuss, in turn, what seem to me to be the main areas of serious concern around AI and its consequences for the future. By its end, I hope you will agree that while things *might* go wrong, they are unlikely to go wrong in the ways that Hollywood imagines.

## EMPLOYMENT AND UNEMPLOYMENT

After the *Terminator* narrative, probably the most widely discussed and widely feared aspect of AI is how it will affect the future of work. Computers don't get tired, don't turn up to work hungover or late, don't argue, don't complain, don't require unions, and perhaps more important, they don't need to be paid. It is easy to see why employers are interested and employees are nervous.

Although "AI Will Make You Redundant" headlines have abounded over the past few years, it is important to understand that what is going on now is nothing new. The large-scale automation of human labor goes back at least to the Industrial Revolution, which took place from about 1760 to 1840. The Industrial Revolution represented a profound change in the way in which goods were manufactured, moving from small-scale production operations ("cottage industries") to large-scale factory production of the type we are familiar with in the present day.

The factory system that was ushered in by the Industrial Revolution brought with it a fundamental change in the nature of work for much of the population. Before the Industrial Revolution, most people were employed, either directly or indirectly, in agriculture. The Industrial Revolution took people out of the countryside, into the towns where factories were located, and moved their jobs from the fields and cottages to the factory floor. The nature of their work changed to the type of job that we still recognize today: working in a factory on a specialized, highly repetitive task, as part of a production process involving a high degree of automation.

There were seismic social changes, which were not universally welcomed. For a few years in the early decades of the nineteenth century, a movement called the Luddites arose—a loosely organized group who rebelled against industrialization, burning and smashing the machines that they saw as taking away their livelihoods. But it was a short-lived movement, stamped out by a fearful British government, who in 1812 made the destruction of machines a crime punishable by death.

Of course, the Industrial Revolution of 1760–1840 was the *first* industrial revolution, because technology has advanced steadily ever since, and there have been similarly seismic changes to the nature of work in the two centuries since the Luddites raged against industrialization. Ironically (and sadly), the same industrial towns that boomed in the first Industrial Revolution were devastated in the late 1970s and early 1980s by another industrial revolution. There were many factors behind the decline of the traditional industries at this time. Globalization of the international economy meant that goods manufactured in the traditional industrial heartlands of Europe and North America were now being produced more cheaply in emerging economies on the other side of the world, and free-market economic policies pioneered by the U.S. and the UK were unfavorable to traditional manufacturing. But the key technological contribution was the development of microprocessors, enabling the automation of vast swathes of unskilled factory jobs across the industrialized world.

While the effects of automation were devastating for many, it is important to remember that the net effect of a new technology like microprocessors will be an *increase* in economic activity.

New technologies create new opportunities for businesses, services, and wealth creation. And this was indeed the case with microprocessors: more jobs and wealth were ultimately created than were destroyed. But by and large, those jobs were not in the traditional industrial centers.

The present concern, of course, is that while previous automation and mechanization largely took the jobs of *unskilled* laborers, perhaps AI will take *skilled* roles. And if it does that, then what roles will be left for people?

That AI will change the nature of work seems certain. What is much less clear is whether the effects will be as dramatic and fundamental as those of the Industrial Revolution or whether they will represent a more modest change.

The debate in this area was galvanized by a 2013 report entitled *The Future of Employment,* written by two colleagues of mine at the University of Oxford, Carl Frey and Michael Osborne.[1] The rather startling headline prediction of their report was that up to 47 percent of jobs in the United States were susceptible to automation by AI and related technologies in the relatively near future.

Frey and Osborne classified 702 occupations according to what they saw as the probability that the job could be automated. The report suggested that those occupations at the highest risk included telemarketers, hand sewers, insurance underwriters, data entry clerks (and indeed many other types of clerk), telephone operators, salespeople, engravers, and cashiers. Those at least risk included therapists, dentists, counselors, physicians and surgeons, and teachers. They concluded, "Our model predicts that most workers in transportation and logistics occupations, together with the bulk of office and administrative support workers, and labor in production occupations, are at risk."

Frey and Osborne also identified three characteristics of jobs that they felt would *resist* automation.

First, perhaps unsurprisingly, they suggested that jobs involving a substantial degree of mental creativity would be safe. Creative professions include the arts, media, and science.

Second, jobs which require strong social skills would be secure too. Jobs that require us to understand and manage the subtleties and complexities of human interaction and human relationships would therefore resist automation.

Finally, they suggested, jobs that involve rich degrees of perception and manual dexterity would be hard to automate. Here the problem for AI is that while great advances have been made in machine perception, humans are much better at it than machines are. We can quickly make sense of highly complex and unstructured environments. Robots can cope with structured and regular environments, but struggle if presented with anything that goes outside the scope of their training. Similarly, the human hand remains far more dexterous than the best robot hand.[2] For the time being, at least, those working in jobs that require a great deal of manual dexterity will likely be safe—any carpenters, electricians, or plumbers reading this book can sleep easily tonight.

While I think the most pessimistic predictions in the report are unlikely to be realized in the medium term, I firmly believe that AI and the associated technologies of advanced automation and robotics will make many people redundant in the near future. If your job involves looking at data on a form and then making a decision (such as whether to give a loan or not), then I'm afraid to say AI is likely to make you redundant. If your job involves talking a customer through a well-defined script (as is the case in many call-center jobs), then I'm sorry that AI will probably make you redundant. If your job involves nothing more than routine driving around a constrained, well-mapped urban area, then it's probable AI will make you redundant. Just don't ask me *when*.

For most of us, however, the main effect of the new technology will be on the *nature* of work that we all do. Most of us won't be replaced by AI systems—we will simply start using AI tools that make us better and more efficient at what we do. After all, the invention of the tractor did not replace farmers: it just made them more efficient farmers. Nor did the invention of the word processor replace secretaries; it simply made them more efficient secretaries. As we go about the endless paperwork and form filling that occupies so much of the working world, we will find ourselves interacting with software agents that can manage and expedite this wearisome process. AI will be embedded with all the tools that we use to carry out our work, making decisions on our behalf in endless ways—many of which will not even be visible. In the words of Andrew Ng, "If a typical person can do a mental task with less than one second of thought, we can probably automate it using AI either now or in the near future."[3] That is a *lot* of tasks.

While many people fear that AI will take all our jobs, leading to a dystopian future of global unemployment and inequality, technological optimists hope that AI, robotics, and advanced automation will lead us to a very different kind of future. These **utopians** believe that AI will free us (at last!) from the drudgery and boredom of work—that in the future, all the work (or at least, all the dirty, dangerous, dreary, or otherwise unpopular work) will be done by machines, leaving us humans free to write poetry, discuss Plato, go mountain climbing, or whatever. This is a beguiling dream, although again not a new one—utopian AI features prominently in science fiction (although, interestingly, not as frequently as *dystopian* AI—perhaps it's harder to write an interesting story about a future in which everyone is happy, healthy, and well educated).

At this point it is useful to reflect on the impact of microprocessor technology when it was developed in the 1970s and early

1980s. As we discussed above, the advent of microprocessors led to a wave of factory automation, and the public debate at that time, about the implications of microprocessor technology, had very much the same flavor as the present debate about the implications of AI. A confident prediction of that period was that, in the not too distant future, we would spend much less of our time in paid employment—three-day workweek, or something like that, would become the norm, and leisure time would expand accordingly.

Things didn't turn out that way. Why not? One theory is that rather than allowing automation, computers, and other technological advances to free up our working hours, we instead worked longer hours to earn more money to pay for more goods and services. So, the argument goes, if we were all prepared to accept simpler lifestyles, with fewer consumer goods and a more basic standard of living, then perhaps we would all have to work less. An alternative explanation is that the economic benefits accruing from automation simply did not get passed on: the rich got richer, and inequality increased. Whatever the precise reasons, the obvious and slightly depressing conclusion from the experience of the 1970s is that for the immediate future at least, technology probably won't create a leisurely utopia for almost all of us.

Important though AI is as a factor in the changing landscape of work, it is by no means the only such factor. It may not even be the most important. For one thing, the inexorable steamroller of globalization has not yet reached the end of its journey, and before it has done so, it will continue to shake up our world in ways we cannot yet envisage. And the computer itself has by no means reached the end of its evolution—for the foreseeable future, computers will continue to get cheaper and smaller and ever-more interconnected, and these developments alone will continue to change our world and the way we live and work in it. And in the background is the ever-changing social, economic, and political landscape of our continuingly more interconnected world: declining fossil fuel resources, climate change, and the rise of populist politics. All these forces will have repercussions for employment and society, and we will feel their effects as much as, if not more than, the effects of AI.

## ALGORITHMIC ALIENATION AND THE CHANGING NATURE OF WORK

You may be surprised (and depending on your worldview, possibly a little disturbed) to see the name Karl Marx in a book about AI, but the coauthor of *The Communist Manifesto* was concerned with issues that are closely related to the current debate about where AI is taking work and society. Of particular relevance is Marx's theory of alienation, which he developed in the middle of the nineteenth century—just after the first industrial revolution. His theory of alienation was concerned with the relationship that a worker has to their work and to society and how the capitalist system affected this relationship. He noted that the workers in the factory system that emerged in the Industrial Revolution were engaged in repetitive, boring, and ultimately unfulfilling jobs, for low wages. They had no opportunity to organize their work; no control over it at all, in fact. This was, Marx argued, an unnatural mode of living. The workers' jobs were, in a very real sense, without meaning; but they had no alternative except to take such unfulfilling and, to them, pointless jobs.

You may well find yourself nodding in recognition at these symptoms. But the rapid development of AI and related technologies exposes a new dimension to Marx's theory, which arises from the possibility that *in the future, our boss could be an algorithm.* Half a century ago, it was not uncommon that the company you worked for when you left school was the company you worked for when you retired. Long-term employment relations were the norm—employees who flitted from one job to another in quick succession were regarded with suspicion.

But long-term employment relationships have become less and less common, replaced by short-term work, piecework, and casual contracts—the gig economy. And one reason why the gig economy has ballooned over the past twenty years is the rise of mobile computing technology, through which large casual workforces can be coordinated on a global scale. The location of a worker at any given time can be monitored by the GPS sensors embedded in their phone, and moment-by-moment instructions can be passed to them via that same phone. Everything they do in their working day, down to the number of keystrokes they type on their computers and the tone of the emails they send, can be monitored and directed, second by second—by a computer program.

One company that has frequently been criticized for its demanding, closely monitored, tightly controlled working environment is Amazon, the online shopping giant. Here is a fairly typical report, from the *Financial Times* in 2013, describing the job of a warehouse worker:[4]

> Amazon's software calculates the most efficient walking route to collect all the items to fill a trolley, and then simply directs the worker from one shelf space to the next via instructions on the screen of the hand-held satnav device. Even with these efficient routes, there's a lot of walking. . . . "You're sort of like a robot, but in human form," said the Amazon [worker]. "It's human automation, if you like."

Had Marx been alive today, he would, I think, have used this report as a perfect illustration of the concept of alienation that he was trying to explain. This is the nightmare of AI-driven automation: human labor is systematically reduced to just those tasks that cannot be automated by machine or software, and what is left is minutely monitored and supervised, with no space for innovation, creativity, individuality, or even for thinking. And imagine how you would feel if your annual appraisal was with a computer program, perhaps even a program that could decide whether to fire you. Somewhat cynically, I am tempted to suggest that we probably shouldn't be too concerned about these problems, though, because the jobs in question won't be around for very long: pretty soon, they will be fully automated by AI, robotics, and advanced automation. (Amazon is investing heavily in warehouse robotics.)

The prospect of a large proportion of the world's working population employed in jobs like this is not an attractive one, although, as I hope should now be clear, it is nothing fundamentally new—it's an AI dimension added to trends that began back in the Industrial Revolution. And of course, many people in the working world today are employed in *far* worse conditions than those of the Amazon warehouse I described above. Technology is neutral about how it is deployed. It is up to employers, governments, unions, and regulators to start thinking about these aspects of AI—how it will affect those in work and what counts as decent working conditions—as well as the issue of unemployment, which has dominated the debate about AI and work to date.

## HUMAN RIGHTS

The discussion above shows how AI systems taking control of our working lives might be deeply alienating. But there are far bigger concerns about the use of AI, which challenge our most fundamental human rights. It is one thing to have an AI system as your boss, telling you when you can and can't take a break, setting you targets, and giving a moment-by-moment critique of your working life; but *what if an AI system had the power to decide whether you went to prison?*

Again, this is not far-fetched—there are AI systems in use today that do something close to this. In the UK, for example, the police force in Durham announced in May 2017 that they would go live with the **Harm Assessment Risk Tool (HART),**[5] an AI system intended to assist police officers in deciding whether someone suspected of a crime should be released or detained in custody. HART is a classic application of machine learning. It was trained on five years of custody data—some 104,000 "custody events"—obtained between 2008 and 2012, and tested with a full year of custody data that was obtained in 2013 (data used in the trial had not been used to train the program)[6]: the system proved to be accurate 98 percent of the time in low-risk cases, and accurate 88 percent of the time with high-risk cases. Interestingly, the system was designed to be cautious with high-risk cases (for example, those involving violent crimes), which explains the discrepancy between the two types of cases. The system was trained using thirty-four different case features. Most of these relate to the suspect's offender history, but the features also include age, gender, and residential address.

There is no suggestion that the Durham police force were delegating all decisions about who should be kept in custody to HART. The system was being used just as a decision support tool, to aid decisions that were being made by custody officers. Nevertheless, there was a good deal of disquiet when the use of HART was made public.

One major concern was that HART looks at a very narrow set of features of a case. It does not have the same understanding of people and processes that an experienced custody officer would. Important decisions are made on the basis of quite narrow data. The lack of transparency about decisions was also a concern (a classic case of a machine learning program apparently being able to perform well without the ability to explain its decisions). And of course, the possibility of bias in the training data and the selected feature set was raised as an issue (and additionally, the fact that the program used a suspect's address as one of the features is of particular concern: the worry is that this will lead to the system being unfair to those from disadvantaged neighborhoods).

Yet another concern was that, even though the tool was intended to *support* decision-making, we might at some point in the future find ourselves in a situation where HART becomes the main decision-maker: a tired, confused, or lazy custody officer might abdicate the responsibility of deciding for themselves and follow HART's recommendation without any further consideration.

But underpinning all these concerns, I think, is the sense that systems like HART erode the role of human judgment. Ultimately, many of us feel more comfortable if we know that a human being is making a decision that has serious consequences for another human being. After all, the fundamental human rights we enjoy, such as the right to trial by our peers, were hard won and are rightly highly prized. Having a computer make a judgment about us, in the way that HART does, perhaps feels like we are discarding these hard-won rights. Such steps should not be taken lightly.

These are all legitimate concerns, although they don't, I think, imply that we should simply introduce a blanket ban on the use of tools like HART. But there are some extremely important caveats concerning their use.

First, as is explicitly intended in the case of HART, such tools should be used for *supporting* human decision-makers rather than replacing them. Machine learning decision-makers are not perfect: they will, from time to time, make decisions that a person would immediately recognize as being nonsensical, and one of the frustrations of current machine learning is that it is hard to identify when they are likely to do this. Blindly following their recommendations in settings that have serious consequences for people is, therefore, profoundly unwise.

Another concern relates to naive development and use of this kind of technology. HART was developed by an experienced research team who appear to have thought carefully about the various different issues that developing such a tool might raise. Not all developers are so experienced or so thoughtful. The worry is, therefore, that systems making important decisions on behalf of people will be built without the care and consideration that went into HART.

HART is just one example of a wide range of systems being put into use by law enforcement agencies, which human rights groups are gravely concerned about. The Metropolitan Police in London have been criticized for using a tool called the Gangs Matrix, a system that has records on thousands of individuals, and plugs this data into a simple mathematical formula to predict the likelihood that these individuals will be involved in gang violence.[7] Much of the Gangs Matrix system seems to be made up of traditional computing technology, and it isn't obvious how much AI is used—but the trend seems clear. Amnesty International described the system as a "racially biased database criminalizing a generation of black men." It has been alleged that doing nothing more than showing a propensity to listen to certain types of music could result in you being listed in the database. In the United States, a company called PredPol sells software to support "predictive policing"—the software is supposed to predict crime hot spot areas.[8] Again, the use of such software raises basic issues of human rights: What if the data is biased? What if the software is poorly designed? What if police forces start to rely on it? Yet another system, COMPAS, aims to predict the likelihood that someone guilty of a crime will reoffend.[9] The system is used to inform sentencing decisions.[10]

An extreme example of how ideas like this can go hopelessly wrong came to light in 2016, when two researchers posted an article in which they claimed to be able to detect criminality *simply by looking at a face.* Such systems take us back to theories about criminality that were discredited a century ago. Subsequent study suggested that the system might be judging criminality on the basis of whether an individual was smiling or not: the people in the police mug shots used to train the system tended not to be smiling.[11]

## KILLER ROBOTS

I have argued—and I hope you will agree—that having an AI system as your boss would be alienating and that having an AI system make decisions such as whether you should be detained in police custody is potentially an affront to your human rights. So how would you feel about an AI program that had the power *to decide whether you lived or died?* As AI has grown in prominence, concerns about this prospect have received a lot of press coverage, fueled at least in part by our old enemy, the *Terminator* narrative.

The topic of autonomous weapons is deeply inflammatory. Many people have extremely strong instinctive views that such systems are repugnant and immoral and should never be built. It often comes as a complete surprise to people holding these views that many other people of good character don't in fact hold the same opinions. So—treading as softly as I can because I know how emotive the subject is—let's dig into the issues raised by the potential of AI-powered autonomous weapons.

Much of the discussion on autonomous weapons has arisen from the increasing use of drones in warfare. Drones are unmanned aircraft, and in military settings, they carry weapons such as missiles. Because they do not have to carry human pilots, drones can be smaller, lighter, and cheaper than conventional aircraft, and because flying them poses no risk to those remotely piloting them, they can be used in situations that would be considered too risky for piloted vehicles. All these features naturally make drones an attractive option for military organizations.

Although there have been several attempts to develop military drones over the last fifty years, it is only in this century that they have become practicable. Since 2001, they have been used in operations in Afghanistan, Pakistan, and Yemen.

Remote-controlled drones raise all sorts of serious ethical issues of their own. For example, since the pilot controlling the drone is in no physical danger, they might choose to take actions that they would not consider if they were physically present and also, just as important in its implications, not take the consequences of their actions as seriously as they would if they were physically present.

For these reasons, and many more, the use of remote-controlled drones is controversial. However, the possibility of *autonomous* drones has raised these concerns to another level. Autonomous drones would not be remotely controlled: they would carry out missions largely without human guidance or intervention. And as part of these missions, they might have the power to decide whether or not to take human life.

The idea of autonomous drones and other varieties of autonomous weapons immediately brings to mind the narrative that you know so well by now: armies of robots killing with relentless, deadly accuracy and without any degree of human mercy, compassion, or understanding. We have already seen why such *Terminator* scenarios are probably not something we should be losing sleep over right now, but the possibility of autonomous weapons going wrong, with lethal consequences, is nevertheless an important argument against their development and use. But there are many other reasons to be concerned about autonomous weapons. One is that a nation possessing such weapons might be less concerned about going to war since their citizens are no longer in the line of fire. Thus, autonomous weapons might make the decision to go to war easier and therefore make warfare more common. But the most common objection is that autonomous weapons are immoral: it is simply wrong to build machines that can decide to take a human life.

It is worth pointing out that AI-powered autonomous weapons are entirely possible now, with current technology. Consider the following scenario:[12]

A small quad-copter drone, of a type that is widely and cheaply available, has been equipped with a camera and GPS navigation, a small onboard computer, and a lump of explosive the size of a hand grenade. The drone has been programmed to traverse the streets of a city, looking for human beings. It does not have to recognize a person, simply identify a human form. And when it identifies a human form, it flies down to it and detonates its explosive.

The AI in this alarming scenario requires only the ability to navigate streets, identify human forms, and fly to them. A competent graduate student of AI, with the right resources, would, I think, be able to build a workable prototype. And these would be *very* cheap to manufacture at scale. Now imagine what would happen if thousands of them were released onto the streets of London, Paris, New York, Delhi, or Beijing. Imagine the carnage; imagine the terror. And for all we know, someone has already built one.[13,14]

While, for many people, there is no rational debate to be had about the merits of autonomous weapons, there is, nevertheless, a debate.

One of the best-known protagonists in this debate is Ron Arkin, a professor at Georgia Tech. He has argued that autonomous weapons are surely inevitable (someone, somewhere, will eventually build them) and that, therefore, the best response is to consider how they might be designed so that they behave *more ethically than human soldiers.*[15] After all, he points out, historically, human soldiers have not had a perfect track record of ethical behavior, and even while "perfect" ethical autonomous weapons are, he acknowledges, impossible, he nevertheless believes we could build autonomous weapons that could, overall, be more ethical than human soldiers.

There are other arguments in support of autonomous weapons. For example, it has been argued that it would surely be better to have robots engage in the vile business of warfare. I have also heard it suggested that it is morally confused to argue against autonomous weapons but not against conventional methods of warfare. For example, when a B-52 bomber releases its bomb load, the bombardier responsible for releasing them doesn't know precisely where the bombs that they have released will land—or on *whom* they will land. So why would one object to autonomous weapons, which explicitly decide who to kill, but *not* object to conventional bombing like this, which *kills at random?* The answer, I suppose, is that one should object to both, but in practice, conventional bombing seems to be less controversial than the idea of lethal autonomous weapons.

Whatever arguments one might try to construct in their favor, my firm impression is that most researchers in the international AI community are strongly against the development of lethal autonomous weapons. The argument that autonomous weapons might be designed to be more ethical than human soldiers is not one that is widely accepted. It is an interesting idea in theory, but in reality, we just don't know how to do it, and it won't be practicable any time soon (see the discussions in the previous chapter). While I daresay this argument was put forward with the best of intentions and also the utmost sincerity, the fear is that it has been hijacked by those who want to justify building autonomous weapons now.

Over the past decade, a movement has emerged among scientists, human rights groups, and others aimed at stopping the development of autonomous weapons. The Campaign to Stop Killer Robots was founded in 2012 and has the backing of major international human rights groups such as Amnesty International.[16] The stated aim of the campaign is to achieve a global ban on the development, production, and use of fully autonomous weapons. The campaign has received a lot of support from the AI community. In July 2015, nearly four thousand AI scientists and more than twenty thousand others signed an open letter in support of a ban; the letter was followed by a number of other similar initiatives, and there are signs that governmental organizations are hearing the concerns being raised. In April 2018, a Chinese delegation to the United Nations proposed a ban on lethal autonomous weapons, and a recent UK government report firmly recommended that AI systems should never be given the power to hurt or kill people.[17]

For reasons that should by now be all too evident, lethal autonomous weapons present dangers as well as moral difficulties. A ban, along the lines of the Ottawa treaty, which bans the development, stockpiling, and use of antipersonnel mines,[18] therefore seems to me to be highly desirable. But this may not be easy: apart from pressure by those groups that seek to build such weapons, *formulating* a ban might not be straightforward. In its 2018 report, the British House of Lords Select Committee on Artificial Intelligence pointed out that it is rather difficult to give a good working definition of a lethal autonomous weapon, and this is going to be a major hurdle for any legislation. And from a purely practical point of view, it would be very hard indeed to try to ban weapons which simply use AI techniques (I would hazard a guess that many conventional weapons systems already use AI software in some form or other). Moreover, banning the use of specific AI technologies, such as neural nets, is unlikely to be enforceable, because software developers can easily disguise the techniques they use in their code.

So even if there is public and political will to control or prohibit the development and use of lethal autonomous weapons, it may be difficult to formulate and implement such legislation. But the good news is that at least there are signs that governments are willing to try.

## ALGORITHMIC BIAS

We might hope that AI systems would be free of the prejudices and biases that plague the human world, but I'm afraid that is not the case. Over the past decade, as machine learning systems have been rolled out into more and more areas of application, we have begun to understand how automated decision-making systems can exhibit **algorithmic bias.** It is now a major research field, with many groups struggling to understand the problems it raises and how to avoid them.

Algorithmic bias, as the name suggests, is concerned with situations in which a computer program—not just AI systems but any computer program—exhibits bias of some form in its decision-making. Kate Crawford, one of the leading researchers in the area, identified two types of harm that may be caused by biased programs.[19]

**Allocative harm** is in evidence when a group is denied (or favored) with respect to some resource. For example, banks might find that AI systems can be useful for predicting whether potential clients are going to be good customers—paying their debts on time and so on. They might train an AI program using records of good and bad customers, and after a while, the AI system might be able to look at the details of a potential customer and predict whether the customer is likely to be good or bad—a classic machine learning application. But if the program is biased, then it might deny mortgages to a certain group or favor another group and grant them. Here, the bias results in an identifiable economic disadvantage (or advantage) for the relevant group.

In contrast, **representation harm** occurs when a system acts to create or reinforce stereotypes or prejudices. One infamous example occurred in 2015, when a Google photo classification system labeled pictures of black people as "gorillas,"[20] thereby reinforcing deeply unpleasant racial stereotypes.

But computers, as we saw earlier, are nothing more than machines for following instructions. So how can they possibly be biased?

The most important single avenue through which bias may be introduced is through data. Machine learning programs are trained using data, and if that data is biased, then the program will learn the bias implicit within the data. Training data can be biased in various ways.

The simplest possibility is when those constructing the data set themselves have a bias. In this case, they will probably embed that bias within the data set. The biases may well not be explicit or conscious. The fact is, however balanced and reasonable we might think we are, we *all* have biases of some form. And these biases will inevitably be manifested in the training data we create.

These issues are all too human, but machine learning can unwittingly help to create biases as well. For example, if the training data for a machine learning program is not representative, then that program will inevitably end up being skewed. (For example, suppose the bank trained its loan software on a data set from one geographical region: then the program might well end up being biased against individuals from other regions.)

Poorly designed programs can also be biased. For example, imagine that, in the banking example above, the key feature of the data that you chose to train your program on was . . . racial origin. Then it would be no surprise if the resulting program made hopelessly biased decisions about who should get a mortgage. (You don't think a bank would be stupid enough to do something like this? Just you wait.)

Algorithmic bias is a particularly prominent issue at present because, as we saw, one feature of the current wave of AI systems is that they are black boxes: they cannot *explain* or *rationalize* the decisions they make in the way that a person can. This problem is exacerbated if we place too much *trust* in the systems we build—and there is anecdotal evidence that we do exactly that with AI systems. Our bank builds their system, runs it on a few thousand examples, and it seems to come up with the same decision that their human experts would make, so they assume it works correctly and rely on it without any further consideration.

It sometimes seems as if every company in the world is frantically rushing to apply machine learning to their business problems. But in this frantic dash, it is all too likely that they will create biased programs, because they don't really understand the issues at stake. And of these, by far the most important is getting the right data.

## DIVERSITY (LACK OF)

When John McCarthy submitted his proposal for the Dartmouth summer school on AI to the Rockefeller Institute, he listed forty-seven individuals whom he wanted to invite to the

event. "Not all of these people came to the Dartmouth conference," he wrote in 1996. "They were the people we thought
might be interested in Artificial Intelligence."

Now, let me ask you a question: How many *women* do you
think attended the Dartmouth event, which saw the founding
of AI as a scientific discipline?

That's right: *none.* I very much doubt that any reputable
contemporary research-funding agency would even consider
supporting an event that failed this most basic of diversity
tests. Indeed, it is standard practice nowadays to require
funding applicants to explicitly address the question of how
they will ensure equality and diversity. But it is, nevertheless, rather striking that the foundation of AI was quite such
a male-dominated affair, and if you have been paying attention throughout this book, you can hardly fail to notice that
AI seems to have remained a largely male-dominated discipline
since then.

While with hindsight we can recognize and regret the in-
equities that were prevalent at the time, I don't think it makes
too much sense to judge an event held in the middle of the
last century using standards that we are still only aspiring to
achieve today. The much more important question is whether
AI today is fundamentally different. And here, while there is
some good news, the overall picture is still somewhat mixed.
On the one hand, if you go to any respected international AI
conference, you will certainly see plenty of female researchers
and researchers from ethnic minorities. But on the other hand,
white males will likely make up the majority: lack of diversity
remains a stubborn problem for AI, as in many areas of science
and engineering.[21]

The gender makeup of the AI community is important for a
whole range of reasons. For one thing, a male-dominated research
community will be off-putting to potential women scientists,

thereby denying the field of valuable talent. But perhaps more important, if AI is solely designed by men, then what we will end up with is, for lack of a better term, *male AI*. What I mean by that is that the systems they build will, inevitably, embody one particular worldview, which will not represent or embrace women. If you don't believe me on this point, then I invite you to read the startling book that opened my eyes to this problem: *Invisible Women* by Caroline Criado Perez.[22] Her key point is that pretty much everything in our world is designed and manufactured with a model of people who reflect just one gender: men. The basic reason for this, she argues, is what she calls the *data gap*: the historical data sets that are routinely used for purposes of manufacturing and design are overwhelmingly male-oriented.

> Most of recorded history is one big data gap. Starting with . . . man the hunter, the chroniclers of the past have left little space for women's role in the evolution of humanity . . . Instead, the lives of men have been taken to represent those of humans overall. When it comes to the lives of the other half of humanity, there is often nothing but silence. . . . These silences, these gaps, have consequences. They impact on women's lives every day. The impact can be minor. Shivering in offices set to a male temperature norm, for example, or struggling to reach a top shelf set at a male height norm. . . . But not life-threatening. Not like crashing a car whose safety measures don't account for women's measurements. Not like having a heart attack go undiagnosed because your symptoms are deemed "atypical." For women in these situations, the consequences of living in a world built around male data can be deadly.

Criado Perez documents, in devastating detail, just how pervasive the problem of male-oriented design and male data really is. For AI, of course, data is essential—but male bias in data sets is ubiquitous. Sometimes, the bias is explicit, such as in the TIMIT spoken-word data set that is widely used to train speech understanding programs. The data set contains 69 percent male voices, with the inevitable consequence that speech understanding systems do a much poorer job of interpreting female voices than male ones. But sometimes, the bias is subtler. Suppose you collect together a set of pictures of kitchens to train your machine learning program, and these pictures predominantly portray women; or suppose that you collect a set of pictures of company CEOs that predominantly portray men. By now, the result will be obvious to you. And furthermore, as Criado Perez points out, both of these things have actually happened.

Sometimes, the bias is embedded within an entire culture. One notorious example was discovered in 2017, when it was revealed that Google Translate sometimes changed genders in text during translation.[23] It turned out that if you translated the English sentences

**He is a nurse.**

**She is a doctor.**

into Turkish, and then back to English, you would end up with

**She is a nurse.**

**He is a doctor.**

No gender stereotypes there, then.

Bias is a problem in AI, but it is a particular problem for women, because the data foundation upon which the new AI is being built has such a strong male bias; and the teams that are building the new AI don't notice this, because they too have a male bias.

One final challenge for AI is that if we build systems that embody certain humanlike features—as we do, for example, when we build software agents like Siri and Cortana—then we might inadvertently build them in such a way as to reinforce gender stereotypes. If we build subservient AI systems that slavishly do our every bidding and we make them look and sound like women, then we will propagate a portrait of women as servants.[24]

## FAKE NEWS

Fake news is precisely what the name suggests: false, inaccurate, or misleading information that is presented as fact. Of course, the world had plenty of sources of fake news before the digital age, but the internet—and more particularly, social media—turned out to be the perfect conduit for the propagation of fake news—and the consequences have been dramatic.

Social media is all about putting people in touch with one another, and modern social media platforms are spectacularly successful at this—Facebook and Twitter in the West and WeChat in China collectively have a sizable proportion of the world's population registered as users. When social media applications first appeared, in the early years of this century, they all seemed to be about friends, family, and everyday life: there were lots of pictures of children and lots of pictures of cats. But social media is a very powerful tool, and it quickly began to be used for other purposes. The phenomenon of fake news, which started to make global headlines in 2016, demonstrated just how powerful social media is and how easily it can be used to influence events on a global scale.

Two events made fake news into global headlines: the U.S. presidential election of November 2016, which led to the election of Donald Trump; and the June 2016 UK national referendum on continued membership of the European Union, which resulted in a narrow vote in favor of leaving. Social media undoubtedly played a significant role in both campaigns—Trump, whatever one thinks of his politics or personal behavior, is adept at using social media to rally his supporters. In both cases, there were suggestions that social media platforms like Twitter had been used to propagate fake news stories favoring the eventual winners.

AI is an important part of the fake news story because it is crucial to the way that fake news is propagated. All social media platforms rely on you spending time interacting with them—it gives them the opportunity to show you advertisements, which is how these platforms ultimately make their money. If you like what you see on the platform, then you are going to spend more time on it than you would do otherwise. So social media platforms have an incentive not to *show you the truth* but to *show you what you like.* How do they know what you like? You tell them, every time you press the Like button. The relevant platform can then look for other similar stories, which you are probably also going to like. A platform that did this well would have built up a (brutally honest) picture of you and your preferences and used this to decide what stories to show you; *John Doe is a white male who likes violent videos and has racist tendencies* . . . What kind of story would the platform show John Doe if it wants him to Like it?

The role of AI in this is to figure out what your preferences are from what you say you like, and perhaps also from the comments that you leave, the links you follow, and so on, and then to find new items that you will also like. These are all classic AI problems, and all social media companies will have teams of researchers and developers working on them.

But if social media platforms behave in this way—figuring out what you like, showing you more of it, and hiding things that you don't like—what sort of picture of the world is social media going to present to John Doe? He is going to see a world of violent videos and racist news stories. He isn't going to get a balanced picture. He will exist in his own social media bubble, and his own skewed view of the world will be reinforced: this is called *confirmation bias*. What makes this so worrying is the scale on which it is happening: social media is manipulating beliefs on a *global scale*, and whether this manipulation is deliberate or purely accidental, this is surely cause for alarm.

In the longer term, AI may have a role to play in changing the way we perceive the world on an even more fundamental level. We each gain information about the world through our senses (sight, hearing, touch, smell, and taste), and collectively, we use this information to build a consensus view of reality: a broadly accepted view of how the world actually is. If you and I both witness a particular event in the same way, then we both get the same information about the event, and we can use this to inform our view of consensus reality. But what happens if there is no common view of the world? What happens if each of us is perceiving the world in a completely different way? AI might make this possible.

In 2013, Google released a wearable computer technology called Google Glass. Resembling everyday spectacles, Google Glass was equipped with a camera and a small projector, providing users with a heads-up display. The glasses connected to a smartphone via a Bluetooth connection. Upon release, there were immediate concerns about the "concealed" camera in Google Glass being used to take pictures in inappropriate situations, but the real potential of the device was in the heads-up display, which could overlay whatever the user was seeing with a projected image. The possible applications were endless. For example, one thing I am personally very bad at is recognizing people: it is a source of continual embarrassment that I meet people I know well but nevertheless struggle to recognize. A Google Glass application that could identify the people I'm looking at and discreetly remind me of their names would be wonderful.

These types of applications are called *augmented reality:* they take the real world and overlay it with computer-generated information or images. But what about apps that do not augment reality but *completely change it* in a way that is imperceptible to users? My son, Tom, is fifteen years old at the time of writing. He is a big fan of J. R. R. Tolkien's *Lord of the Rings* books and the films that were made from them. Imagine a Google Glass app that altered his view of school so that his friends looked like elves and his schoolteachers looked like orcs. You might have a similar *Star Wars*–themed app and so on. This would be great fun, but here is the thing: What does consensus reality mean if we are all inhabiting our own private worlds? You and I would no longer have common, shared experiences upon which to build a consensus. And of course, such applications can be *hacked.* Imagine that Tom's glasses were hacked so that his beliefs were being manipulated *directly* by fundamentally altering the way in which he was perceiving the world.

Although applications like this are not possible at present, they have a good chance of becoming possible within the next two or three decades. We already have AI systems that can generate images that appear, to humans, to be utterly real, but which in fact have been entirely constructed by a neural network. At the time of writing, for example, there is a lot of concern about DeepFakes.[25] These are pictures or videos that have been altered by a neural network to include people who were not present in the original. DeepFakes have been used to alter pornographic videos too, inserting "actors" into the video who did not in fact participate.[26]

At the time of writing, the quality of DeepFake videos is comparatively poor, but it is steadily getting better, and soon, we won't be able to tell whether a photo or video is real or a DeepFake. At that point, the principle that photos or videos provide a reliable record of events will no longer be viable. If we each inhabit our own AI-powered digital universe, there is a real danger that societies, built on common values and principles, will start to fracture. Fake news on social media is just the beginning.

## FAKE AI

We saw in chapter 4 how software agents like Siri, Alexa, and Cortana emerged in the first decade of this century as a direct descendent of research on agents in the 1990s. Shortly after Siri emerged, a number of stories appeared in the popular press, reporting some undocumented features of the system. You could say to Siri things like, "Siri, you're my best friend," and Siri would come back with what looked like a meaningful response (I just tried it: "Okay, Michael. I'll be your friend, in fair weather and foul"). The press were all agog. Is this general AI? they wondered. Well, no. Predictably, all Siri was doing was pulling out a stock response to certain key words and statements—pretty much just what ELIZA was doing decades earlier. There is no intelligence at work there at all. The apparently meaningful answers were nothing more than fake AI.

Apple is not the only company guilty of producing fake AI. In October 2018, the British government announced that a robot called Pepper would give evidence in the Houses of Parliament.[27] But it was nonsense. The robot Pepper was certainly present (and for the record, it is a fine robot, with a lot of wonderful research behind it). But Pepper simply answered predetermined questions with answers that had been prewritten for it. This was not even at the level of ELIZA.

There was no intent to deceive in the Siri or Pepper incidents—they were both a good-natured bit of fun. But many in the AI community were annoyed, because they paint a completely false picture of what AI is all about. For one thing, if anybody watching the Pepper show thought that the robot was *really* answering the questions that were being posed, then they would be left with a completely misleading view of what was currently possible with AI-based question-answering systems. But I doubt many people were taken in—it wasn't hard to see what was really going on, and the problem then is that people might think this kind of nonsense is what AI is actually all about: fakery.

A similar incident occurred in December 2018, when a "hi-tech robot" dancing at a youth science forum in Yaroslavl, Russia, turned out to be . . . a man in a robot suit.[28] It is unclear whether the organizers of the event intended to deceive, so let's give them the benefit of the doubt. But Russian state television reported the "robot" as if it were the real thing. Anybody watching might reasonably have concluded that this represented the current state of the art in robotics and AI.

Unfortunately, fakery like this is all too common on the fringes of AI, to the intense frustration of AI researchers. In October 2017, Saudi Arabia announced that it had granted citizenship to a robot called Sophia, and the announcement, unsurprisingly, garnered a lot of media attention.[29] Many commentators highlighted the irony of the announcement (giving citizenship to a machine), given Saudi Arabia's less-than-ideal track record on human rights, and women's rights in particular.

Fake AI, then, is where people are misled into believing that what they are seeing is AI when in fact there are human minds behind the scenes. I've heard rumors that AI start-up companies who can't get their technology to work for a crucial demo will resort to fake AI behind the scenes. I have no idea how widespread this practice is, but fake AI is a real problem for everyone and a massive irritation for the AI community.

# 9

## Conscious Machines?

IF I HAVE succeeded in doing one thing in this book, I hope it is to have convinced you that, while the recent breakthroughs in AI and machine learning are real and exciting, they are not a silver bullet for general AI. Deep learning may be an important ingredient for general AI, but it is by no means the only ingredient. Indeed, we don't yet know what some of the other ingredients are, still less what the recipe for general AI might look like. All the impressive capabilities we have developed—image recognition, language translation, driverless cars—don't add up to general intelligence. In this sense, we are still facing the problem that Rodney Brooks highlighted back in the 1980s: we have some *components* of intelligence but no idea how to build a system that integrates them. And in any case, some of the key components are still missing: as we have seen, even the best of contemporary AI systems cannot exhibit any meaningful *understanding* of what they are doing. For all that they may excel at what they do, they are nothing more than software components optimized to carry out a specific narrow task.

Since I believe we are a long way from general AI, it naturally follows that I should be even more dubious about the prospects for strong AI: the idea of machines that are, like us, conscious, self-aware, truly autonomous beings. Nevertheless, in this final chapter, let's indulge ourselves. Even though strong AI is not anywhere in prospect, we can still have some fun thinking about it and speculating about how we might progress toward it. So let's take a trip together down the road to conscious machines. We'll imagine what the landscape might look like, which obstacles we might meet, and what sights we can expect to see on the way. And crucially, we'll talk about how we can know when we're near the end of the road.

## CONSCIOUSNESS, MIND, AND OTHER MYSTERIES

In 1838, the British scientist John Herschel carried out a simple experiment in an attempt to find out how much energy was being radiated by our sun. He exposed a container of water to sunlight and measured how long it took for the sun's energy to raise the temperature of the water in the container by one degree Celsius. A simple calculation then allowed Herschel to estimate how much energy our star emits every second. The results were beyond comprehension: in one second, the sun radiates unimaginable quantities of energy—an inordinately larger amount than is generated on earth in a whole year. But this created a scientific conundrum: emerging geological evidence indicated that our world (and hence our sun) was tens of millions of years old, at least, but there was no known physical process that could power the sun for such huge periods of time. Any known source of energy would result in the sun burning out in, at most, a few thousand years. Scientists of the time flailed around, inventing charmingly implausible theories in an attempt to reconcile the evidence of a simple, easily repeatable experiment with the evidence of the geological record. In the event, it was not until the end of the nineteenth century, and the emergence of nuclear physics, that scientists began to understand the ferocious powers latent within the atomic nucleus. It was a whole century after Herschel's experiment before physicist Hans Bethe was finally able to present what is now the widely accepted account of energy production in stars, by means of nuclear fusion.[1]

When we turn to strong AI—the goal of building machines that *really have* conscious minds, self-awareness, and understanding, in much the same way as we do—we find ourselves in the same position as scientists of Herschel's time were: the phenomena of mind and consciousness in people—how they evolved, how they work, and even the functional role that they play in our behavior—are as utterly mysterious to us now as the forces that powered the sun were to scientists then. We don't have answers to any of these questions, and no answers are in immediate prospect for any of them. At present, we have nothing more than a few clues and a great deal of speculation. Indeed, satisfactory answers to these questions would be up there with understanding the origins and fate of the universe in terms of scientific significance. It is this fundamental lack of understanding that makes strong AI so difficult to approach—we have no idea where or how to begin.

In fact, the situation is worse than this, because we don't even really know what we are dealing with. I have casually thrown around terms like *consciousness, mind,* and *self-awareness,* but we don't, in truth, know what these things are. They *seem* like obvious concepts—we all experience them, after all—but we don't have the scientific apparatus to talk about any of them. We can't be certain in a scientific sense that they are even real, for all the common-sense evidence of our personal experiences. Herschel was able to approach his problem with an experiment, using well-understood, measurable physical concepts: temperature, energy, and so on. We just don't have tests like these available to study consciousness or mind: they aren't amenable to objective observation or measurement. There is no standard scientific unit of measurement for mind or subjective experience, or even any direct way of measuring them—*I* can't see what *you* are thinking or experiencing. Historically, much of our understanding of the structure and operation of the human brain was obtained by studying people whose brains had been damaged in some way, by disease or trauma—but this hardly lends itself to a systematic research program. While neuroimaging techniques such as magnetic resonance imaging (MRI) give us important insights into the structure and operation of the brain, they don't provide access to an individual's mind.

Despite the fact that we don't have any precise definitions, we can identify some common features that arise in discussions about consciousness.

Probably the most important idea is that something conscious must have the ability to *experience things subjectively*. By *subjectively*, I mean *from your own personal mental perspective*. One important aspect of this is the sensation of internal mental phenomena—what philosophers call **qualia.** This is a fancy name for a simple idea: qualia are the mental sensations that we all experience, like the smell of coffee. Pause for a moment and think about that smell, or better, go and make yourself a good cup. Inhale the aroma. That sensation you experienced was an example of qualia. The experience of drinking a cold beer on a hot day; the feeling when the weather begins to change from winter to spring; the feeling when my children succeed at something new. All of these are qualia: you may well recognize them and have enjoyed them yourself—but the paradox is that, even though we believe we are talking about the same experiences, there is no way that we can know whether you experience them in the same way that I do, because qualia—and other mental experiences—are inherently *private*. The mental experience *I* had when *I* smelled the coffee was only accessible to *me*; I have no way of telling whether *you* actually had a similar experience, even if we use the same words to describe it.

One of the most famous contributions to the debate on consciousness was made by the American philosopher Thomas Nagel in 1974.[2] Nagel proposed a test by which, he suggested, you can distinguish whether something is or is not conscious. Suppose you want to know whether the following are conscious:

- **A human being**
- **An orangutan**
- **A dog**
- **A rat**
- **An earthworm**
- **A toaster**
- **A rock**

The test Nagel proposed was to consider whether the question "What is it like to be an *X*?" makes sense when applied to entities like those above. If we believe that it is like something to be an *X* (where *X* is a human being or an orangutan, etc.), then Nagel argued that the *X* in question is conscious. Looking at our list above, the question is meaningful when applied to human beings. What about orangutans? I think so, and the same for dogs and also (although slightly less obviously) rats. So orangutans, dogs, and rats, according to Nagel's test, are conscious. Of course, this is not a "proof" that they are conscious—we are having to rely on common sense rather than objective scientific evidence.

What about earthworms? Here, I think we are at the threshold of consciousness. Earthworms are such simple creatures that it seems doubtful (to me, anyway) that Nagel's test makes sense in this case: so by his argument, earthworms are not conscious. There is some scope for debate in this latter case—one might argue that even earthworms have some primitive consciousness, but then I would have to insist that it was indeed primitive compared to human consciousness. However, I'm not going to allow debate about toasters and rocks: they obviously fail the test. It isn't *like anything* to be a toaster.

Nagel's test highlights a number of important points.

First, *consciousness is not an all-or-nothing thing*. It is a spectrum, with fully fledged human consciousness at one extreme and earthworms at the other. But even between humans, there are differences. The extent to which a person is conscious will vary depending on whether they are under the influence of alcohol or drugs or are just plain tired.

Second, consciousness is *different* for different entities. The title of Nagel's article was "What Is It Like to Be a Bat?" Nagel chose bats for the title of his article because they are so unlike us. Nagel's question surely makes sense when applied to bats, so bats enjoy consciousness, according to Nagel's theory. But bats have senses that we don't have, most notably a kind of sonar. They emit ultrasonic sounds as they fly and detect the echoes of these squeaks to perceive their environment. Some bats are even able to detect the earth's magnetic field and use it for navigation—they have their own built-in magnetic compass. We don't have these senses, and for this reason, we cannot actually imagine what it is like to be a bat, even though we think Nagel's question is meaningful when applied to bats. So bat consciousness is thus different from human consciousness. In fact, Nagel believed it is beyond our ability to comprehend, even though we may be confident it exists.

Nagel's main purpose was to set out a test for consciousness ("What is it like to be an *X*?") and to argue that certain forms of consciousness must remain beyond our comprehension (we can't imagine what it would be like to be a bat). But his test can be applied to computers, and most people seem to believe that it isn't *like anything* to be a computer, any more than a toaster.

For this reason, Nagel's "What is it like" argument has been used against the possibility of strong AI. Strong AI is impossible, according to this argument, because computers cannot be conscious by Nagel's argument. I am personally not convinced by this argument, because asking "What is it like to be a . . ." is, for me, nothing more than an appeal to our intuition. Our intuition works well at separating out the obvious cases—orangutans and toasters—but I don't see why we should expect it to be a reliable guide in the more subtle cases or cases that are far outside our own experience of the natural world—such as AI. Perhaps we can't imagine what it would be like to be a computer just because they are so utterly unlike us. But that doesn't imply (to me, at least) that machine consciousness is impossible—just that machine consciousness would be *different*.

Nagel's argument is one of many that have been set out in an attempt to show strong AI to be impossible. Let's take a look at the best-known of these.

## IS STRONG AI POSSIBLE?

Nagel's argument is closely related to a common-sense objection to the possibility of strong AI, which says that it is not possible because *there is something special about people*. This intuitive response starts from the view that computers are different from people because people are animate objects but computers are not. According to this argument, I have more in common with a rat than with a computer; a computer has more in common with a toaster than with me.

My response to this is that however remarkable humans are, ultimately, they are nothing more than a bunch of atoms. People and their brains are physical entities, obeying physical laws—even if we don't yet quite know what those laws are. Humans are remarkable, wonderful, incredible things, but from the point of view of the universe and its laws, we are nothing special. Of course, this doesn't answer the difficult question of *how* a particular bunch of atoms leads to conscious experience—a point to which we will return later.

A variation of the "humans are special" argument was put forward by the American philosopher Hubert Dreyfus, whom we met earlier as a critic of early AI. One of Dreyfus's main points in his critique of AI was that it had rather oversold itself, considering its actual achievements, and in this respect, he surely had a point. But he also had a concrete argument against the possibility of strong AI. His argument was that much of human action and decision-making is based on "intuition," which he believed could not be made precise in the way that computers require. In short, Dreyfus argued, human intuition could not be reduced to a recipe like a computer program.

Now, there is certainly a wealth of evidence that much of our decision-making is not based on explicit or rigorous reasoning.[3] We frequently make decisions without being able to articulate our rationale for them; probably most of our decision-making is of this type, in fact. In this sense, we certainly use some sort of intuition. But surely this results from experience we have gained over time (or perhaps experience learned through evolution, which has been transmitted to us through our genes), which, even if we cannot articulate it at a conscious level, is nevertheless nothing mysterious. And as we have seen, computers can learn from experience and become effective decision-makers, even if they cannot articulate the rationale for their decisions.

The most famous argument against the possibility of strong AI is due to the philosopher John Searle, who coined the terms *strong* and *weak AI*. He invented a scenario called the **Chinese**

**room** in an attempt to show that strong AI is impossible. The Chinese room scenario goes like this:

Imagine a man working alone in a room. Through a slot in the door, he receives cards on which questions are written in Chinese; he understands no Chinese himself. He takes these cards and then carefully follows a list of written instructions in order to write an answer in Chinese, which he then passes back out of the room. Now, the room (and its contents) is actually engaged in a Chinese Turing test, and the answers provided by the room convince the interrogators that the subject of the test is a human.

Now, ask yourself: *Is there any understanding of Chinese present here?* Searle argues not. The man in the room doesn't understand Chinese, and surely the room itself has no understanding of Chinese. No matter where we look here, we find no understanding of Chinese. The man is doing nothing more than carefully following a precise recipe to derive a response to the question. His human intelligence is used only to the extent that he dutifully follows the instructions he is given.

Observe that the man is doing exactly what a computer does: simply following a list of instructions—a recipe. The "program" he is executing are the instructions he is given. So according to Searle, by the same argument, a computer passing the Turing test will not exhibit understanding.

If Searle's argument is correct, then it means that understanding—and hence strong AI—cannot be produced by following a recipe. Strong AI, therefore, can't be achieved with conventional computers. If correct, this simple argument would kill the grand dream of AI. No matter how much your program *appeared* to have understanding, this would be nothing more than an illusion: behind the scenes, there would be nothing there.

Many counterarguments have been proposed to Searle's critique.

An obvious common-sense response is to point out that Searle's Chinese room is simply not possible. Apart from anything else, having a human play the role of a computer processor would mean it would take millennia to carry out a single second's worth of computer program instructions, and the idea of encoding the relevant program as written instructions is absurd: a typical large-scale computer program of the present day will involve about a hundred million lines of computer code. (To actually write out such code in a form that a human could read would require tens of thousands of printed volumes.) A computer can retrieve instructions from memory in microseconds, whereas the Chinese room computer would be billions of times slower. Given these practical facts, the Chinese room and its contents *could not* convince an interrogator that it was a person: it could *not*, in fact, pass the Turing test.

Another standard response to the Chinese room is that while the person in the room does not exhibit understanding and the room itself doesn't, the *system* that must be present, which contains the person, the room, the instructions, and so on, *does*. And indeed, if we went digging around in a human brain, looking for understanding, we would not find it. While there certainly are areas of the human brain that seem to be responsible for language understanding, we will not find, within these, understanding of the kind Searle asks for.

I believe that there is an even simpler response to Searle's ingenious thought experiment. The Chinese room puzzle, expressed as a kind of Turing test, is a cheat because it does not treat the room as a black box. We only claim that there is no understanding in the Chinese room when we start to look inside it. The Turing test itself insisted that we should only look at the inputs and outputs and ask whether the behavior we witness is indistinguishable from that of a human. It seems to me to be pointless to get caught up in an argument about whether a computer "really" understands if, in fact, it is doing something that is indistinguishable from human understanding.

Another argument against the possibility of strong AI is that there is some particular feature of human brains or bodies that creates human consciousness and self-awareness and which cannot be realized by a computer. What might such a feature be? The distinguished British physicist Roger Penrose argued that consciousness might have its origins in certain quantum phenomena, which by their very nature cannot be computed using conventional computers. (The details of why certain quantum phenomena cannot be computed need not detain us here.) Penrose's argument is an intriguing one, and nobody has come up with a definitive rebuttal—but equally, there doesn't seem to be any actual evidence that consciousness does indeed depend on non-computable quantum phenomena. The mainstream AI community doesn't give this argument much credence, although technically it is considered possible.

Yet another possible objection is that perhaps intelligence cannot be computed by a conventional computer because of their mathematically provable limitations. Remember that we know, from Turing's work, that there are fundamental limits to what computers can and cannot do—there are some clearly definable problems that cannot be solved by a computer. So, *what if intelligent behavior of the kind that AI strives for is not computable in the sense that Turing proposed?* Turing himself discussed this as a possible argument against strong AI. Most AI researchers aren't concerned by it, but as we have often seen earlier, the problem of what is *practically* computable has been a major stumbling block for AI throughout its history.

## MIND AND BODY

We now turn to the most famous philosophical puzzle in the study of consciousness: the **mind-body problem.** Certain physical processes in the human body and brain give rise to the conscious mind—but how and why, exactly, do they do that? What precisely is the relationship between the physical world of neurons, synapses, and axons to our conscious subjective experience? This is one of the biggest and oldest problems in science and philosophy; the Australian philosopher David Chalmers called it the **hard problem of consciousness.**

The literature on the topic goes back at least as far as Plato. In the *Phaedrus,* he proposed a model of human behavior in which a reasoning component of the brain acts as a charioteer holding the reins of two horses—one horse representing rational, noble desires, the other representing irrational or unworthy desires. The course that a person takes through life depends on how their charioteer controls these two horses. A similar idea appears in the Hindu Upanishads.[4]

Viewing the rational self as a chariot driver is a wonderful metaphor. But cute though it undoubtedly is—I'm rather taken with the idea of holding the reins to both the noble and unworthy parts of my mind—it suffers from a common problem in theories of the mind. Plato imagines the charioteer to be a mind, but all he's then done is say that the mind is controlled by *another mind* (the charioteer). Philosophers call this the **homunculus problem**—*homunculus* means "little man," the "little man" in this case being the charioteer. It's a problem because it doesn't actually explain anything—it just delegates the problem of "mind" to another representation of the mind.

In any case, the "chariot" model is dubious because it suggests that *reasoning* is the main driver for our behavior, and there is a wealth of evidence that this is very much not the case. For example, in a celebrated series of experiments, the neuroscientist John-Dylan Haynes was apparently able to detect decisions made by human subjects up to *ten seconds* before the subjects themselves were consciously aware that they had made a decision.[5]

This result raises all sorts of questions, but one of the most important is simply, if conscious thought and reasoning is not the mechanism via which we decide what to do, then what on earth is it *for*?

When we are presented with some feature of the human body, evolutionary theory tells us that we should ask what evolutionary advantage that feature gave us. So in just the same way, we can ask what evolutionary advantage the conscious mind gave us. Because, presumably, if it gave us *no* advantage, then it wouldn't have come into being.

One theory is that the conscious mind is actually nothing more than a meaningless by-product of the features in our body that *actually* produce our behavior. This theory goes by the rather exhausting name of **epiphenomenalism.** If the conscious mind is epiphenomenal, then rather than being the charioteer holding the reins, as Plato suggested, your conscious mind is, instead, a *passenger* in the chariot, *under the illusion that it is the charioteer.*

A slightly less dramatic view is that the conscious mind does not play a primary role in our behavior in the way that Plato suggested, but rather that it somehow arises from other processes in our brain—presumably, processes that are not present in lower-order animals, which, insofar as we can tell, don't enjoy as rich a mental life as we do.

In what follows, we'll explore one key component of our conscious human experience: our social nature, by which I mean our ability to understand ourselves and others as part of a social group and to be able to reason about others and about how others see us. This key capability most probably evolved as a requirement for living and working together in large, complex social groups. To understand this, we'll start by looking at a celebrated thread of work on the social brain carried out by the British evolutionary psychologist Robin Dunbar.

## THE SOCIAL BRAIN

Dunbar was interested in the following simple question: Why do humans (and other primates) have such large brains,[6] compared with those of other animals? Ultimately, the brain is an information-processing device and one that consumes a considerable proportion of the total energy produced by a human body—about 20 percent is a typical estimate. So a large brain would have evolved in order to deal with some important information-processing requirement for the primate—and given its energy requirements, it would have to yield some substantial evolutionary advantage. But what information-processing requirement and what evolutionary advantage, exactly?

Dunbar looked at a number of primates and possible factors that might imply the need for enhanced information-processing capacity. For example, one possible explanation might be the primate's need to keep track of food sources in their environment. Another possible explanation could be the requirement for primates with a larger ranging or foraging area to keep track of bigger spatial maps. However, Dunbar found that the factor that best predicted brain size was the primate's **mean social group size:** the average number of animals in that primate's social groups. But this, then, suggests that the large brain size of primates is needed to be able to successfully maintain large social groups—more precisely, the need to keep track of, maintain, and exploit the social relationships in these groups.

Dunbar's research raised a tantalizing question: Given that we know the average human brain size, what does his analysis predict as being the average group size for humans? The value obtained by this analysis is now known as *Dunbar's number,* and it is usually quoted as 150. That is, given the average human brain size and Dunbar's analysis of other primates, we would expect the average size of human social groups to be around

150. Dunbar's number might have remained a curiosity but for the fact that subsequent research found that this number has arisen repeatedly, across the planet, in terms of actual human social group sizes. For example, it seems that Neolithic farming villages typically contained around 150 inhabitants. Of more recent interest is the fact that Dunbar's number has something to say about the number of friends we actively engage with on social networking sites such as Facebook.

Dunbar's number can be interpreted as being roughly the number of human relationships that a human brain can manage. Of course, most of us nowadays interact with much larger groups than this—but Dunbar's number is the number of relationships that we can truly keep track of.

In short, if this analysis is correct, then the *human* brain is different because it is a *social* brain. It is large, compared to that of other primates, because we live in large social groups, and this requires the ability to keep track of and manage a large number of social relationships.

The natural next question is what it means, exactly, to keep track of and manage these social relationships. To answer this, we will explore an idea due to the celebrated American philosopher Daniel Dennett—the idea that we understand and predict people's behavior using what he called the **intentional stance.**

## THE INTENTIONAL STANCE

As we look around our world and try to make sense of what we see, it seems that we naturally make a distinction between agents and other objects. We have already seen the term *agent* used in this book: it was the idea of an AI program independently acting on our behalf, rationally pursuing our preferences. An agent in the sense that we are now discussing is something that seems to have a similar status to us, as a self-determining actor. When a child deliberates over which chocolate to choose from a selection and carefully picks one, we perceive agency: there is choice and deliberate, purposeful, autonomous action. In contrast, when a plant grows from underneath a rock and, over time, pushes the rock to one side, we see no agency: there is action, of a kind, but we perceive neither deliberation nor conscious purpose in the action.

So why do we interpret the actions of the child to be those of an agent but the actions of a plant growing to be a mindless process?

To understand the answer to this question, think about the various different kinds of explanation that are available to us when we try to explain the processes changing our world. One possibility is to understand the behavior of an entity with reference to what Dennett calls the **physical stance.** With the physical stance, we use the laws of nature (physics, chemistry, etc.) to predict how a system will behave. For example, Dennett suggests that when he releases a stone he has been holding in his hand, he uses some simple physics (the stone has weight, it is acted upon by the force of gravity) to predict, successfully, that the stone will fall to the ground. Now, while the physical stance works well in cases such as this, it is of course not practicable for understanding or predicting the behavior of *people,* who are far too complex to be understood in this way. It might be possible in principle (we are, ultimately, just a bunch of atoms) but of course isn't remotely feasible in practice. Nor, for that matter, is it a very practicable way of understanding the behavior of computers or computer programs—the source code for a typical modern computer operating system will run to hundreds of millions of lines.

Another possibility is the **design stance,** in which we predict behavior based on our understanding of the purpose that a system is supposed to fulfill—what it was designed for. Dennett gives the example of an alarm clock. When someone presents us with an alarm clock, we do not need to make use of physical laws in order to understand its behavior. If we know it to be a clock, then we can interpret the numbers it displays as the time, because clocks are designed to display the time. Likewise, if the clock makes a loud and irritating noise, we can interpret this as an alarm that was set at a specific time, because making loud and irritating noises at specified times (but not otherwise) is again something that alarm clocks are designed to do. No understanding of the clock's *internal mechanism* is required for such an interpretation—it is justified by the fact that alarm clocks are designed to exhibit such behavior.

A third possibility, and the one that interests us here, is the one that Dennett calls the **intentional stance**.[7] From this perspective, we attribute **mental states** to entities—mental states such as beliefs and desires—and then use a common-sense theory of these mental states to predict how the entity will behave, under the assumption that it makes choices in accordance with its attributed beliefs and desires. The most obvious rationale for this approach is that when explaining human activity, it is often useful to make statements such as the following:

> **Janine *believes* it is going to rain and *wants* to stay dry.**
>
> **Peter *wants* to finish his marking.**

If Janine believes it is going to rain and wants to stay dry, then we might predict that she will wear a raincoat or take an umbrella, or avoid going outside altogether, for these are the kinds of behaviors that we expect of a rational agent who has these beliefs and desires. Thus, the intentional stance has both explanatory and predictive power: it allows us to explain what people did and what they will (be likely to) do.

Note that, as with the design stance, the intentional stance is neutral about the *internal mechanism* that is actually producing the behavior. The theory works equally well for machines as for people, as we will discuss in more detail below.

Dennett coined the term **intentional system** to describe entities whose behavior can be most usefully understood and predicted by the method of attributing to them beliefs, desires, and rational choice.

There is a natural hierarchy of increasingly sophisticated intentional systems. A first-order intentional system has beliefs and desires of its own, but it doesn't have any beliefs and desires *about* beliefs and desires. In contrast, a second-order intentional system is capable of having beliefs and desires *about* beliefs and desires. The following statements illustrate this:

> **First order:** Janine *believed* it was raining.
>
> **Second order:** Michael *wanted* Janine to *believe* it was raining.
>
> **Third order:** Peter *believed* Michael *wanted* Janine to *believe* it was raining.

In our everyday lives, it seems we probably do not use more than about three layers of the intentional stance hierarchy (unless we are engaged in an artificial intellectual activity, such as solving a puzzle), and it seems that most of us struggle to go beyond fifth-order reasoning.

Our use of the intentional stance is intimately bound to our status as social animals. The role of such intentional ascriptions seems to be to enable us to understand and predict the behavior of other agents in society. In navigating our way through our complex social world, we become involved in higher-order intentional thinking, whereby the plans of individuals (whether ourself or those we observe) are influenced by the anticipated intentional behavior of other agents. The value of such thinking is clear from its ubiquity in human life and the extent to which we take it for granted in our communications. Recall the six-word conversation between Alice and Bob that we saw in chapter 1:

Bob: I'm leaving you.
Alice: Who is she?

The obvious intentional stance explanation of this scenario is simple, uncontrived, and compelling: Alice *believes* that Bob *prefers* someone else to her and that he is *planning* accordingly; Alice also *wants* to *know* who this is (perhaps in the *hope* of dissuading him), and she *believes* that asking Bob will induce him to tell her. It is difficult to explain the exchange *without* appealing to concepts like belief and desire, not only as playing a role in Alice's and Bob's behavior but also featuring explicitly in their thinking and planning.

Dunbar looked at the relationship between brain size and the capacity for higher-order intentional reasoning capabilities in humans and other animals. It turns out that the capability for higher-order intentional reasoning is, approximately speaking, a linear function of the relative size of the frontal lobe of the brain. Since brain size correlates strongly with social-group size, it follows that a natural evolutionary explanation for large brains is precisely the need for, and value of, social reasoning—higher-order intentional reasoning—within a complex society. Whether hunting in groups, battling with conflicting tribes, pursuing a mate (perhaps against rivals), or gaining allies for influence and leadership, the value of being able to understand and anticipate the thinking of other individuals is self-evident. Returning to Dunbar's arguments, larger social groups will make more demands for higher-order social reasoning, thereby explaining the relationship between brain size and social-group size that Dunbar identified.

Going back to our original motivation, levels of intentionality appear to correlate with degrees of consciousness. As we already discussed, the class of things we would admit as *first-order* intentional systems is very broad indeed. But higher-order intentionality is a much higher bar. We are higher-order intentional systems, but I would not accept anybody trying to persuade me that (for example) an earthworm was. What about a dog? You might just about be able to persuade me that a dog was capable of having beliefs about my desires (it believes I want it to sit, for example)—but if a dog is capable of higher-order intentional reasoning, then it is likely to be, at most, a rather limited and specialized capability. There are indications that some other primates have a limited capacity for higher-order intentional reasoning. For example, vervet monkeys make use of a warning cry to indicate the presence of leopards to other monkeys (a threat to the monkey community). They have been observed to use the warning cry to trick other vervet monkeys into believing that they are under attack by leopards.[8] A natural explanation of this trick seems to involve higher-order intentional reasoning: "If I make the warning cry, then they will *believe* leopards are attacking and *want* to get away." One can, of course, put forward alternative explanations, which do not imply higher-order intentional reasoning. Nevertheless, the anecdote gives credence to the claim that some nonhuman animals do engage in higher-order intentional reasoning.

Social reasoning, in the form of higher-order intentionality, seems to be correlated with consciousness, and social reasoning evolved to support complex social networks and large social groups. But why might social reasoning require consciousness, in the form of there being "something it is like" to be an agent? My colleague Peter Millican has suggested that the answer may lie precisely in the computational efficiency of the intentional stance. If I have conscious access to *my own* functional motivators—in the form of desires, beliefs, and so on—and can also think myself into the subjective situation of other people, then this enables me to predict their behavior (in both actual and imagined circumstances) far more efficiently than I could otherwise. By imagining myself in your position if I were to steal your food, for example, I can instinctively *feel* (without calculation) the sort of anger you would then feel, can anticipate the reprisals you might plan, and will thus be motivated to resist my temptation to steal from you. This is an interesting speculation, but whatever the relationship may be between *human* social reasoning ability and consciousness, we aren't likely to get definitive answers any time soon. So let's now return to our main purpose, AI, and consider the possibility of *machines* that are capable of social reasoning.

## CAN MACHINES BELIEVE AND DESIRE?

The intentional stance plays an important role in human society, but it can also be applied to a wide range of other entities. For example, consider a conventional light switch. The intentional stance provides a perfectly serviceable descriptive explanation for the behavior of a light switch: the switch transmits current when it believes we want it transmitted and not otherwise; we communicate our desires by flicking the switch.[9]

However, the intentional stance is surely not the most *appropriate* way of understanding and predicting the behavior of a light switch: here it is far simpler to adopt the physical stance or the design stance. By contrast, an intentional stance explanation of the switch's behavior requires attributing to it beliefs about the flowing or absence of current and also beliefs about our own desires. Although this intentional account provides an accurate prediction of the switch's behavior, it seems rather extravagant as an *explanation*.

With respect to the intentional stance applied to machines, there seem to be two main questions: When is it *legitimate* to use the intentional stance to talk about machines, and when is it *useful* to do so? John McCarthy, who was an influential thinker on the subject of machines with mental states, had this to say on these questions:[10]

> To ascribe certain beliefs, knowledge, free will, intentions, consciousness, abilities or wants to a machine or computer program is legitimate when such an ascription expresses the same information about the machine that it expresses about a person. . . . Ascription of mental qualities is most straightforward for machines of known structure such as thermostats and computer operating systems, but is most useful when applied to entities whose structure is very incompletely known.

This is a rather dense quote, so let's try to unpack it a little bit. First, McCarthy suggests, an intentional stance explanation of a machine should express the same information about the machine that it expresses about a person. This is quite a big requirement, of course—reminiscent of the indistinguishability requirement for the Turing test. Adapting an example we saw earlier, if we claim a robot believes it is raining and that the robot wants to stay dry, then this would be a meaningful ascription if the robot behaved as a rational agent with these beliefs and desires would behave. So if the robot was able to, then it should take appropriate action to prevent getting wet. If the robot didn't take such action, then we would be inclined to say that either it didn't believe it was raining, or it didn't really want to stay dry, or that it was not rational.

Finally, McCarthy points out that the intentional stance is of greatest value when we don't understand the structure or operation of an entity. It provides a method for explaining and predicting behavior independently of its internal structure and operation (for example, whether it is a person or a dog or a robot). If you are a rational agent with the desire to stay dry and the belief that it is raining, then I can explain and predict your behavior without knowing anything else about you.

## TOWARD CONSCIOUS MACHINES

What does all this tell us with respect to our dreams for AI? Let me conclude by rashly making some concrete proposals for what progress toward conscious machines might look like and how we might create it. (I look forward to rereading this section in my dotage, to see how my predictions turn out.)

Let's go back to DeepMind's celebrated Atari-playing system. Recall that DeepMind built an agent that learned to play a large number of Atari video games. These games were in many ways relatively simple, and of course, DeepMind has subsequently progressed beyond these to much more complex games such as *StarCraft II*.[11] At present, the main concerns in experiments like this are: to be able to handle games with very large branching factors; games in which there is imperfect information about the state of the game and the actions of other players; games where the rewards available in the game are distant from the actions that lead to those rewards; and games where the actions an agent must perform are not simple binary decisions, such as in *Breakout*, but ones which involve long and complex sequences, possibly coordinated with—or in competition with—the actions of others.

This is fascinating work, and the progress that's been made here is very impressive. But it is hard to see a simple progression of this work leading to conscious machines, because the issues being addressed don't seem to be those that are relevant for consciousness (this is not a criticism of this work, of course; these are just not the issues that this work aims to address).

Given our discussion above, let me therefore make some tentative suggestions about how we might progress toward this goal. Suppose we have a machine learning program that learns—on its own, just as the DeepMind agent did in *Breakout*—to succeed in a scenario that requires *meaningful, complex higher-order intentional reasoning.* Or a scenario that requires an agent to *tell a sophisticated lie,* which implies higher-order intentional reasoning. Or a scenario in which an agent learns to communicate and meaningfully express properties of its own mental state and those of others. A system that could learn to do these things in a meaningful way would, I think, be some significant way along the road to conscious machines.[12]

What I have in mind here is something like the **Sally–Anne test,** which has been proposed to assist in the diagnosis of autism in children.[13] Autism is a serious, widespread psychiatric condition that manifests itself in childhood:[14]

> The key symptoms [of autism] are that social and
> communication development are clearly abnormal in
> the first few years of life, and the child's play is charac-
> terized by a lack of the usual flexibility, imagination and
> pretense. . . . The key features of the social abnormalities
> in autism . . . include lack of eye contact, lack of normal
> social awareness or appropriate social behavior, "alone-
> ness," one-sidedness in interaction and inability to join a
> social group.

A typical Sally–Anne test consists of a short story that is told or enacted to the child being tested, such as this one:

Sally and Anne are in a room, which contains a basket, a box, and a marble. Sally puts the marble into the basket and then leaves the room. While Sally is out of the room, Anne takes the marble out of the basket and puts it into the box. Then Sally comes back into the room and wants to play with the marble.

The child being tested is then asked a question: "Where will Sally look for the marble?"

The appropriate answer to this question is "In the basket."

But to get to this answer, the subject would need to be able to do some reasoning about the beliefs of others: Sally did not see Anne move the marble, so Sally will believe that the marble is where she left it—in the basket. Autistic children, it seems, overwhelmingly answer the question incorrectly, while neuro-typical children almost always answer correctly.

Simon Baron-Cohen and his coauthors, who pioneered this approach, take this as evidence that autistic children lack what has become known as a **theory of mind (ToM).** The ToM is the practical, common-sense capability that fully developed adults have, to be able to reason about the mental states—beliefs, de-sires, and so on—of others and themselves. Humans are not born with a ToM, but neurotypical humans are born with the capability to develop one. Clinically normal children develop their theory of mind progressively: by the age of four, children are able to reason including others' perspectives and viewpoints, and their ToM is fully developed in their teens.

At the time of writing, there is beginning to be some re-search into how machine learning programs can learn a primi-tive ToM.[15] Researchers recently developed a neural net system called ToMnet ("theory of mind net"), which is able to learn how to model other agents and behave correctly in situations resem-bling Sally–Anne puzzles. However, the work is at a very early stage, and the ability to solve a Sally–Anne puzzle is not enough to claim artificial consciousness. But this is, I think, a step in the right direction. It gives us another goal to aim toward: an AI system that autonomously learns a human-level ToM.

## WOULD IT BE LIKE US?

When discussing AI and people, we talk about the brain a lot. And this is quite natural: the brain is the main information-processing component of the human body, which does the heavy lifting when we carry out tasks such as solving problems, understanding stories, and so on. So we naturally tend to imagine that the brain is like the computer controlling a driverless car, receiving and interpreting sensory information from our eyes and ears and other senses, and telling our hands, arms, and legs what to do. But that is a grossly oversimplified model of the true state of affairs, because the brain is one component of a tightly integrated system containing multiple complex components, which evolved together as a single organism over the billions of years since life first appeared on our planet. We are, in evolutionary terms, nothing more than apes—apes with a sense of entitlement—and human consciousness has to be understood against this background.

Our current capabilities—including the conscious mind—are the result of evolutionary forces that drove the development of our ancestors.[16] Just as our hands and eyes and ears evolved, so did human consciousness. Fully fledged human consciousness did not emerge overnight: there was no sudden "light switch" moment, before which our ancestors were like earthworms and after which they were like Shakespeare. Our ancient ancestors did not enjoy the full range of conscious experience that we did, and we are most likely not enjoying the same range of conscious experiences that our descendants in the deep future will. The process of evolutionary development is surely not finished yet.

Intriguingly, the historical record can give us some clues about how and why certain elements of consciousness emerged. The historical record is sparse, so we are inevitably forced to speculate—a lot—but nevertheless, the clues are tantalizing.

Every currently existing species of ape—including *Homo sapiens* (us)—had a common ancestor until about eighteen million years ago. Around that time, the evolutionary family tree of the apes began to fork, sending orangutans on a different evolutionary path about sixteen million years ago and separating us from gorillas and chimpanzees between six and seven million years ago. After this split, our ancestors began to adopt a characteristic that distinguished us from other ape species: we began to spend more time on the ground rather than in trees, ultimately walking upright on two feet. One possible explanation for this transformation is that it was necessitated by climactic changes, which reduced forest cover, forcing our tree-dwelling ancestors out into open land. Leaving tree cover probably increased the risk of attack by predators, and a natural evolutionary response was to increase the size of social groups, since larger social groups are less susceptible to predator attack. And larger social groups demanded the social-reasoning skills we discussed earlier and larger brains to support these social-reasoning skills.

Although our ancestors used fire sporadically as far back in time as a million years ago, it seems that it became commonly used somewhere approximately half a million years ago. Fire gave a whole range of benefits to our ancestors—it gave light and warmth, frightened away potential predators, and increased the opportunities for feeding. However, fires require care and maintenance—so this new technology required the ability to cooperate in order to take turns minding the fire, collecting fuel, and so on. Cooperation of this kind would have benefited from the ability to undertake higher-order intentional reasoning (in order to understand each other's desires and intentions) and possibly language, which seems to have evolved at about the same time. Once the capability for language was established, further benefits from its development would have become apparent.

We can't reconstruct with any certainty the precise sequence of developments, and the new capabilities they would have brought with them, but the broad sweep seems clear; and I think we can make out some components of consciousness appearing over time. Of course, this doesn't answer the hard problem of consciousness—but at least it gives us some plausible clues about how and why some of the necessary components for fully fledged human consciousness appeared. Ultimately, they might turn out to be dead ends, but conjecture usually leads toward a more solid understanding—eventually. And they offer more than simply treating consciousness as an unknowable mystery.

At some point in the future, we will understand consciousness, just as we now understand the forces that power the sun. At that point in time, much of the current debate on the subject will probably seem as quaintly amusing as the various theories put forward to explain the source of the sun's power did before nuclear physics provided the answers.

Suppose we succeed in my research agenda, of building machines with a human-level theory of mind; machines that autonomously learn to handle complex higher-order intentional reasoning, that can build and maintain complex social relationships, that can express complex properties of their own mental state and those of others. Would these machines *really* have a "mind," consciousness, self-awareness? The problem is, from this distance, we just can't answer this question—we'll have a much better idea as we get closer to being able to build such machines. If, that is, we *are* ever able to build them.

It may conceivably be that we are *never* able to answer this question satisfactorily, although I can see no reason why this should be the case. But at this point, the ghost of Alan Turing is trying to get my attention. Because Turing, you may recall, argued that if the machine is doing something that is really *indistinguishable* from the "real thing," then we should stop arguing about whether it is "really" conscious or self-aware. If it is truly indistinguishable, by any reasonable test that we can invent, then that may be as much as we can ever ask.

# Acknowledgments

I WOULD LIKE to thank George Lucas at InkWell Management for representing me in the U.S. and Bryn Clark at Flatiron for giving me the chance to publish with her.

Special thanks to: Ian J. Goodfellow, Jonathon Shlens, and Christian Szegedy for their permission to use the "panda/gibbon" images that appear in chapter 5, from their paper "Explaining and Harnessing Adversarial Examples"; Peter Millican for permission to adapt some material from a paper we wrote together; Subbarao Kambhampati for useful feedback on some of my main arguments and pointing me toward Pascal's wager; Nigel Shadbolt for discussion, encouragement, and fantastic anecdotes about the history of AI; and Reid G. Smith for his permission to adapt some of his teaching materials relating to the MYCIN system.

I am grateful to those colleagues, students, and unlucky acquaintances who read drafts of the book at short notice and gave enormously valuable feedback. Thanks here to Ani Calinescu,

Tim Clement-Jones, Carl Benedikt Frey, Paul Harrenstein, Andrew Hodges, Matthias Holweg, Will Hutton, Graham May, Aida Mehonic, Peter Millican, Steve New, André Nilsen, James Paulin, Emma Smith, Thomas Steeples, André Stern, John Thornhill, and Kiri Walden. Naturally, any errors that surely remain are entirely my responsibility.

I am honored to acknowledge the support of the European Research Council under Advanced Grant 291528 (RACE), which funded me and my research group from 2012 to 2018. My work on RACE was made infinitely more productive and immensely more pleasurable by an energetic, brilliant, and endlessly supportive research group led by Julian Gutierrez and Paul Harrenstein. I very much hope we will continue to collaborate far into the future.

Finally, I am enormously grateful to my agent, Felicity Bryan, who made this book possible, and gave me every encouragement throughout its gestation. Sadly, Felicity passed away in June 2020. She was a truly remarkable individual, a force of nature. It is hard to believe she is gone. Carrie Plitt at Felicity Bryan Associates was presented with the unenviable task of picking up the reins on my projects after Felicity passed away; she did so with grace and charm, for which I am very grateful.

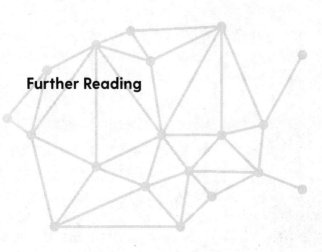

## Further Reading

THE DEFINITIVE MODERN academic introduction to AI is Stuart Russell and Peter Norvig's *Artificial Intelligence: A Modern Approach*, 3rd ed. (Essex, UK: Pearson, 2016). For a detailed history and the field up to about 2010, written by one of the field's greatest researchers, see Nils Nilsson's *The Quest for Artificial Intelligence* (New York: Cambridge University Press, 2010). The best text on the "new" AI is *Deep Learning* by Ian Goodfellow, Yoshua Bengio, and Aaron Courville (Cambridge, MA: MIT Press, 2017).

Many contemporary articles in AI and machine learning are deposited in an open online archive called arXiv. Articles within the arXiv are referenced with a simple numbering scheme thus: arXiv:1412.6572. You can obtain the relevant article by going to https://arxiv.org and entering the relevant reference number (in this case, 1412.6572).

# Notes

## Introduction

[1] Catherine Clifford, "Google CEO: A.I. Is More Important Than Fire or Electricity," CNBC, February 1, 2018, www.cnbc.com/2018/02/01/google-ceo-sundar-pichai-ai-is-more-important-than-fire-electricity.html.

[2] E. Kumar Sharma, "AI Is the New Electricity, Says Coursera's Andrew Ng," *Business Today,* March 5, 2018, www.businesstoday.in/opinion/interviews/ai-is-the-new-electricity-says-courseras-andrew-ng/story/271963.html.

## Chapter 1: Turing's Electronic Brains

[1] Andrew Hodges, *Alan Turing: The Enigma* (London: Burnett Books, 1983).

[2] Quite apart from his astonishing scientific legacy, Turing had a profound social legacy within the United Kingdom. Following a lengthy high-profile public campaign, the government posthumously pardoned him in 2014; shortly after, pardons were issued to all men who had been prosecuted under the same law.

[3] This is the most obvious recipe for checking primality but by no means the most elegant or efficient. A neat alternative called the *sieve of Eratosthenes* has been known since antiquity.

[4] At this point I'll stop distinguishing between *universal Turing machines* and *Turing machines* and simply refer to *Turing machines*.

[5] Strictly speaking, an algorithm is a recipe, and a program is an algorithm that has been encoded in an actual programming language like Python or Java. Thus, algorithms are independent of programming languages.

[6] Turing machines actually require a much cruder form of programming than this. The instructions I've listed here are typical of a relatively low-level programming language, but still much more abstract (and much easier to understand) than a Turing machine program.

[7] Thomas H. Cormen, Charles E. Leiserson, and Ronald L. Rivest, *Introduction to Algorithms*, 1st ed. (Cambridge, MA: MIT Press, 1990).

[8] A. M. Turing, "Computing Machinery and Intelligence," *Mind* 59, no. 236 (1950): 433–60.

[9] Ernest Davis, "Collection of Winograd Schemas," NYU, https://cs.nyu.edu /faculty/davise/papers/WinogradSchemas/WS.html.

[10] Unfortunately, the terminology in the literature is imprecise and inconsistent. Most people seem to use *artificial general intelligence* to refer to the goal of producing general-purpose human-level intelligence in machines, without being concerned with philosophical questions such as whether they are self-aware. In this sense, artificial general intelligence is roughly the equivalent of Searle's weak AI. However, just to confuse things, sometimes the term is used to mean something much more like Searle's strong AI. In this book, I use it to mean something like weak AI, and I will just call it *general AI*.

[11] Human Brain Project, www.humanbrainproject.eu/en.

## Chapter 2: The Golden Age

[1] One of the most influential of these was due to John McCarthy himself: an idea called *time-sharing*. He realized that when someone was using a computer, most of the time the computer was actually idle, waiting for them to type something or run a program. He discovered that it would be possible for many people to use a computer at the same time by switching attention between users during these idle periods: you get the benefit of my idle time, I get the benefit of yours. It made for much more efficient use of expensive computers.

[2] It actually stands for *List Processor*. LISP is all about *symbolic* computation and lists of symbols are the key to that.

[3] J. McCarthy et al., "A Proposal for the Dartmouth Summer Research Project on Artificial Intelligence, 1955," *AI Magazine* 27, no. 4 (2006): 12–14.

[4] Terry Winograd, *Understanding Natural Language* (Orlando, FL: Academic Press, 1972).

[5] In linguistics, the use of words like *it*, *her*, and *she* to refer to things that appeared previously in a dialogue is called *anaphora*. A computer program trying to understand or build a natural-language dialogue has to be able to resolve such references—it remains a challenge to the present day, and SHRDLU's ability to cope with (limited) anaphora was regarded as groundbreaking.

[6] R. E. Fikes and N. J. Nilsson, "STRIPS: A New Approach to the Application of Theorem Proving to Problem Solving," *Artificial Intelligence* 2, no. 3–4 (1971): 189–208.

[7] The computer that controlled SHAKEY was a PDP-10, a state-of-the-art mainframe computer from the late 1960s. It weighed more than a ton and required a large room to house it. A PDP-10 could be equipped with up to about a megabyte of memory; the smartphone in my pocket has about four thousand times more memory and is inconceivably faster.

[8] This isn't intended to be a precise calculation—just an approximate value to give us some idea of the scale of the numbers involved.

[9] Technically, let $b$ be the branching factor of the search problem, and let $d$ be the depth of the search tree. Then the bottom level of the tree (at depth $d$) will contain $bd$ states, where $bd$ is $b$ to the power of $d$, that is:

> The branching factor exhibits what is technically called **exponential growth.** Some references use the term **geometric growth,** although I don't think I've ever seen this term used in the AI literature.

[10] I have simplified the statement of the traveling salesman problem in the main text a little. A more precise textbook definition is as follows:

> We are given a list of cities, $C$, and for each pair of cities $i$ and $j$ in $C$, we are given a distance, $d_{i,j}$. Thus, $d_{i,j}$ is the distance between $i$ and $j$. We are also given a "bound," $B$, which is the total distance that we can travel on a single tank of fuel. The question we have to answer is whether there is a tour of all the cities (that is, some way that the cities, $C$, can be ordered) so that by traveling from each city to the next in the order defined in this way, and then at the end, returning to the starting city, we travel no more than the total distance $B$.

[11] *P* stands for *polynomial*—a feasible algorithm to solve a problem is one that has "polynomial running time."

## Chapter 3: Knowledge Is Power

[1] Patrick Winston and Berthold Horn, *LISP,* 3rd ed. (Essex, UK: Pearson, 1989).

[2] Edward H. Shortliffe, *Computer-Based Medical Consultation: MYCIN* (New York: American Elsevier, 1976).

[3] John McCarthy, "Concepts of Logical AI" (unpublished note).

[4] R. V. Guha and D. Lenat, "Cyc: A Midterm Report," *AI Magazine* 11, no. 3 (1990).

[5] Vaughan Pratt, "CYC Report" (unpublished note, April 16, 1994), Stanford University, http://boole.stanford.edu/cyc.html.

[6] R. Reiter, "A Logic for Default Reasoning," *Artificial Intelligence* 13, no. 1–2 (1980): 81–132.

[7] This example is called the *Nixon diamond*: a standard pictorial representation of the scenario has a diamond shape.

## Chapter 4: Robots and Rationality

[1] Interestingly, these higher aspects of human intelligence are handled by a part of the brain called the *neocortex*, and the record of human evolution tells us that this part of the brain evolved only relatively recently. Reasoning and problem solving are quite new capabilities for people: our ancestors coped without them for most of evolutionary history.

[2] iRobot, www.irobot.com.

[3] Rodney A. Brooks, "A Robot That Walks: Emergent Behaviors from a Carefully Evolved Network," in *Proceedings of the 1989 Conference on Robotics and Automation* (Scottsdale, AZ: 1989).

[4] S. Vere and T. Bickmore, "A Basic Agent," *Computational Intelligence* 6, no. 1 (1990): 41–60.

[5] P. Maes, "Agents That Reduce Work and Information Overload," *Communications of the ACM* 37, no. 7 (1994): 30–40.

[6] John von Neumann and Oskar Morgenstern, *Theory of Games and Economic Behavior* (Princeton, NJ: Princeton University Press, 1944).

[7] To make this simple, I'm equating money and utility here. In practice, money and utility are often related, but they are not usually the same, and you will annoy a lot of economists if you assume that utility theory is simply concerned with money. In fact, utility theory is just a numeric way of capturing and computing with preferences.

[8] Stuart Russell and Peter Norvig, *Artificial Intelligence—A Modern Approach*, 3rd ed. (Essex, UK: Pearson, 2016), 611.

[9] Robin R. Murphy, *An Introduction to AI Robotics* (Cambridge, MA: MIT Press, 2001).

[10] Bart Selman, Hector J. Levesque, and David G. Mitchell, "A New Method for Solving Hard Satisfiability Problems," in *Proceedings of the Tenth National Conference on AI (AAAI 1992)* (San Jose, CA: 1992).

## Chapter 5: Deep Breakthroughs

[1] Accounts in the press vary on the amount paid for the DeepMind acquisition. The figure of £400 million ($650 million U.S.) was reported in: Samuel Gibbs, "Google Buys UK Artificial Intelligence Startup DeepMind for £400m," *Guardian,* January 27, 2014, www.theguardian.com/technology/2014/jan/27/google-acquires-uk-artificial-intelligence-startup-deepmind.

[2] Marvin Minsky and Seymour Papert, *Perceptrons: An Introduction to Computational Geometry* (Cambridge, MA: MIT Press, 1969).

[3] David E. Rumelhart and James L. McClelland, eds., *Parallel Distributed Processing,* 2 vols. (Cambridge, MA: MIT Press, 1986).

[4] D. E. Rumelhart, G. E. Hinton, and R. J. Williams, "Learning Representations by Back-Propagating Errors," *Nature* 323, no. 6088 (1986): 533–6.

[5] Ian Goodfellow, Yoshua Bengio, and Aaron Courville, *Deep Learning* (Cambridge, MA: MIT Press, 2016).

[6] Looking at the historical rate of increase in the number of neurons, we might expect to reach the same number of artificial neurons as a human brain in about forty years or so. That does not mean, though, that artificial neural nets will achieve *human level intelligence* in forty years, because the brain is not simply a big neural network. It also has structure.

[7] ImageNet, www.image-net.org.

[8] WordNet, Princeton University, https://wordnet.princeton.edu.

[9] A. Krizhevsky, I. Sutskever, and G. E. Hinton, "ImageNet Classification with Deep Convolutional Neural Networks," *NIPS* 25 (2012): 1106–14.

[10] I. Goodfellow et al., "Explaining and Harnessing Adversarial Examples," arXiv:1412.6572.

[11] V. Mnih et al., "Playing Atari with Deep Reinforcement Learning," arXiv:1312.5602v1.

[12] V. Mnih et al., "Human-Level Control Through Deep Reinforcement Learning," *Nature* 518, no. 7540 (2015): 529–33.

[13] D. Silver et al., "Mastering the Game of Go with Deep Neural Networks and Tree Search," *Nature* 529, no. 7587 (2016): 484–9.

[14] *AlphaGo*, directed by Greg Kohs (New York: Moxie Pictures, 2017).

[15] D. Silver et al., "Mastering the Game of Go Without Human Knowledge," *Nature* 550, no. 7676 (2017): 354–9.

[16] CaptionBot, www.captionbot.ai.

[17] Google Translate, https://translate.google.com.

[18] This translation is by the Scottish writer and translator C. K. Scott Moncrieff. His translation of *À la recherche du temps perdu* is one of the most celebrated translations in literary history: his translation is regarded as a masterpiece, although it has been criticized for taking liberties with Proust's language.

### Chapter 6: AI Today

[1] Pallab Ghosh, "First Ever Black Hole Image Released," BBC News, April 10, 2019, www.bbc.co.uk/news/science-environment-47873592.

[2] James Vincent, "These Faces Show How Far AI Image Generation Has Advanced in Just Four Years," *Verge*, December 17, 2018, www.theverge.com/2018/12/17/18144356/ai-image-generation-fake-faces-people-nvidia-generative-adversarial-networks-gans.

[3] Ian Sample, "Google's DeepMind Predicts 3D Shapes of Proteins," *Guardian*, December 2, 2018, www.theguardian.com/science/2018/dec/02/google-deepminds-ai-program-alphafold-predicts-3d-shapes-of-proteins.

[4] This figure would have been rather skewed by the proportion of people dying either in childbirth or in the early years of their life—someone making it into adulthood would have stood a fair chance of living to what we would now regard as a reasonable age.

[5] "John Hancock Adds Fitness Tracking to All Policies," BBC News, September 20, 2018, www.bbc.com/news/technology-45590293.

[6] J. De Fauw et al., "Clinically Applicable Deep Learning for Diagnosis and Referral in Retinal Disease," *Nature Medicine* 24, no. 9 (2018): 1342–50.

[7] Andreas Herrmann, Walter Brenner, and Rupert Stadler, *Autonomous Driving* (Bingley, UK: Emerald, 2018).

[8] Ford, www.ford-mobility.eu/autonomous-vehicles.

[9] "Rio Tinto's Autonomous Haul Trucks Achieve One Billion Tonne Milestone," Rio Tinto, January 30, 2018, www.riotinto.com/media/media-releases-237 _23991.aspx.

### Chapter 7: How We Imagine Things Might Go Wrong

[1] Andrew Griffin, "Facebook's Artificial Intelligence Robots Shut Down After They Start Talking to Each Other in Their Own Language," *Independent,* July 31, 2017, www.independent.co.uk/life-style/gadgets-and-tech/news/facebook -artificial-intelligence-ai-chatbot-new-language-research-openai-google -a7869706.html.

[2] Ray Kurzweil, *The Singularity Is Near* (New York: Penguin, 2005).

[3] Vernor Vinge, "The Coming Technological Singularity: How to Survive in the Post-Human Era," in *Vision 21: Interdisciplinary Science and Engineering in the Era of Cyberspace* (Cleveland, OH: NASA Lewis Research Center, 1993), 11–22.

[4] T. Walsh, "The Singularity May Never Be Near," arXiv:1602.06462v1.

[5] *I, Robot,* directed by Alex Proyas (Los Angeles: Twentieth Century Fox, 2004).

[6] Daniel S. Weld and Oren Etzioni, "The First Law of Robotics (A Call to Arms)," in *Proceedings of the National Conference on Artificial Intelligence (AAAI-94)* (San Jose, CA: 1994), 1042–7.

[7] P. Foot, "The Problem of Abortion and the Doctrine of the Double Effect," *Oxford Review* 5 (1967).

[8] Gus Lubin, "Self-Driving Cars Are Already Deciding Who to Kill," *Business Insider,* December 29, 2016, www.businessinsider.com/self-driving-cars -already-deciding-who-to-kill-2016-12?r=UK.

[9] "Asilomar AI Principles," Future of Life Institute, https://futureoflife.org/ai -principles.

[10] In the interests of transparency, I should point out that I was invited to both of the meetings that led to the Asilomar principles, and I would have loved to have gone. As it happens, on both occasions, prior commitments got in the way.

[11] "Responsible AI Practices," Google AI, https://ai.google/responsibilities/responsible-ai-practices.

[12] "Draft Ethics Guidelines for Trustworthy AI," European Commission, December 18, 2018, https://ec.europa.eu/digital-single-market/en/news/draft-ethics-guidelines-trustworthy-ai.

[13] "The IEEE Global Initiative on Ethics of Autonomous and Intelligent Systems," IEEE, https://standards.ieee.org/industry-connections/ec/autonomous-systems.html.

[14] Virginia Dignum, *Responsible Artificial Intelligence* (Cham, Switzerland: Springer, 2019).

[15] Nick Bostrom, *Superintelligence* (Oxford, UK: Oxford University Press, 2014).

[16] Andrew Y. Ng and Stuart Russell, "Algorithms for Inverse Reinforcement Learning," in *Proceedings of the Seventeenth International Conference on Machine Learning (ICML '00)* (Burlington, MA: Morgan Kaufmann Publishers, 2000).

## Chapter 8: How Things Might Actually Go Wrong

[1] C. B. Benedikt Frey and M. A. Osborne, "The Future of Employment: How Susceptible Are Jobs to Computerization?," *Technological Forecasting and Social Change* 114 (January 2017).

[2] Rodney Brooks's blog, https://rodneybrooks.com/blog.

[3] Andrew Ng, "What Artificial Intelligence Can and Can't Do Right Now," *Harvard Business Review,* November 9, 2016, https://hbr.org/2016/11/what-artificial-intelligence-can-and-cant-do-right-now.

[4] Sarah O'Connor, "Amazon Unpacked," *Financial Times,* February 8, 2013, www.ft.com/content/ed6a985c-70bd-11e2-85d0-00144feab49a.

[5] Chris Baraniuk, "Durham Police AI to Help with Custody Decisions," BBC News, May 10, 2017, www.bbc.co.uk/news/technology-39857645.

[6] M. Oswald et al., "Algorithmic Risk Assessment Policing Models: Lessons from the Durham HART Model and 'Experimental' Proportionality," *Information & Communications Technology Law* 27, no. 2 (2018): 223–50.

[7] Peter Yeung, "The Grim Reality of Life Under Gangs Matrix, London's Controversial Predictive Policing Tool," *Wired*, April 2, 2019, www.wired.co.uk /article/gangs-matrix-violence-london-predictive-policing.

[8] PredPol, www.predpol.com.

[9] "Northpointe Suite Case Manager," Equivant, www.equivant.com/northpointe -suite-case-manager.

[10] Ed Yong, "A Popular Algorithm Is No Better at Predicting Crimes Than Random People," *Atlantic*, January 17, 2018, www.theatlantic.com/technology /archive/2018/01/equivant-compas-algorithm/550646.

[11] "Criminal Machine Learning," Calling Bullshit, www.callingbullshit.org /case_studies/case_study_criminal_machine_learning.html.

[12] I believe this scenario is due to Stuart Russell.

[13] Zak Doffman, "Russian Military Plans Swarms Of Lethal 'Jihadi-Style' Drones Carrying Explosives," *Forbes*, July 8, 2019, www.forbes.com/sites /zakdoffman/2019/07/08/russias-military-plans-to-copy-jihadi-terrorists-and -arm-domestic-size-drones/#1dfa1ca032e7.

[14] David Hambling, "Turkish Military to Receive 500 Swarming Kamikaze Drones," *Forbes*, June 17, 2020, www.forbes.com/sites/davidhambling/2020 /06/17/turkish-military-to-receive-500-swarming-kamikaze-drones.

[15] Ronald Arkin, "Governing Lethal Behavior: Embedding Ethics in a Hybrid Deliberative/Reactive Robot Architecture," technical report GIT-GVU-07-11, College of Computing, Georgia Institute of Technology, Atlanta, GA.

[16] Campaign to Stop Killer Robots, www.stopkillerrobots.org.

[17] House of Lords Select Committee on Artificial Intelligence, report of Session 2017–19, *AI in the UK: Ready, Willing and Able?*, HL Paper 100, April 2018.

[18] International Campaign to Ban Landmines, www.icbl.org/en-gb/home .aspx.

[19] Ayesha Bajwa, "What We Talk About When We Talk About Bias (A Guide for Everyone)," *Medium*, August 17, 2019, https://medium.com/@ayeshar bajwa/what-we-talk-about-when-we-talk-about-bias-a-guide-for-everyone -3af55b85dcdc.

[20] Richard Nieva, "Google Apologizes for Algorithm Mistakenly Calling Black

People 'Gorillas,'" CNET, July 1, 2015, www.cnet.com/news/google-apologizes -for-algorithm-mistakenly-calling-black-people-gorillas.

[21] Holly Else, "Can a Major AI Conference Shed Its Reputation for Hosting Sexist Behaviour?," *Nature*, November 27, 2018, www.nature.com/articles/d41586 -018-07552-1.

[22] Caroline Criado Perez, *Invisible Women: Exposing Data Bias in a World Designed for Men* (London: Chatto & Windus, 2019).

[23] James Zou and Londa Schiebinger, "AI Can Be Sexist and Racist—It's Time to Make It Fair," Stanford University, July 18, 2018, https://history.stanford .edu/news/ai-can-be-sexist-and-racist-%E2%80%94-it%E2%80%99s-time -make-it-fair.

[24] Kaitlyn Barclay, "The Future of AI Is Genderless," *Fast Company*, March 18, 2019, www.fastcompany.com/90320194/the-future-of-ai-is-genderless.

[25] Oscar Schwartz, "You Thought Fake News Was Bad? Deep Fakes Are Where Truth Goes to Die," *Guardian*, November 12, 2018, www.theguardian.com /technology/2018/nov/12/deep-fakes-fake-news-truth.

[26] Alex Hern, "AI Used to Face-Swap Hollywood Stars into Pornography Films," *Guardian*, January 25, 2018, www.theguardian.com/technology/2018/jan/25/ai -face-swap-pornography-emma-watson-scarlett-johansson-taylor-swift-daisy -ridley-sophie-turner-maisie-williams.

[27] "Pepper the Robot Appears Before Education Committee," UK Parliament, October 12, 2018, https://committees.parliament.uk/committee/203/education -committee.

[28] Andrew Roth, "'Hi-Tech Robot' at Russia Forum Turns Out to Be Man in Suit," *Guardian*, December 12, 2018, www.theguardian.com/world/2018/dec /12/high-tech-robot-at-russia-forum-turns-out-to-be-man-in-robot-suit.

[29] Zara Stone, "Everything You Need to Know About Sophia, the World's First Robot Citizen," *Forbes*, November 7, 2017, www.forbes.com/sites/zarastone /2017/11/07/everything-you-need-to-know-about-sophia-the-worlds-first -robot-citizen/#cdc677c46fa1.

## Chapter 9: Conscious Machines?

[1] John N. Bahcall, "How the Sun Shines," Nobel Prize, www.nobelprize.org /prizes/themes/how-the-sun-shines-2.

[2] T. Nagel, "What Is It Like to Be a Bat?," *Philosophical Review* 83, no. 4 (1974): 435–50.

[3] Daniel Kahneman, *Thinking, Fast and Slow* (New York: Farrar, Straus and Giroux, 2011).

[4] "He who has the understanding of the driver of the chariot and controls the rein of his mind, he reaches the end of the journey, that supreme abode of the all-pervading" (Katha Upanishad, 1.3).

[5] C. S. Soon et al., "Unconscious Determinants of Free Decisions in the Human Brain," *Nature Neuroscience* 11, no. 5 (2008): 543–5.

[6] More precisely, it was *neocortex* size that Dunbar was interested in. The neocortex is the part of the brain that deals with perception, reasoning, and language.

[7] Daniel C. Dennett, *The Intentional Stance* (Cambridge, MA: MIT Press, 1987).

[8] D. C. Dennett, "Intentional Systems in Cognitive Ethology," *Behavioral and Brain Sciences* 6, no. 3 (1983): 342–90.

[9] Y. Shoham, "Agent-Oriented Programming," *Artificial Intelligence* 60, no. 1 (1993): 51–92.

[10] John McCarthy, "Ascribing Mental Qualities to Machines," in *Formalizing Common Sense: Papers by John McCarthy*, ed. V. Lifschitz (Norwood, NJ: Alblex, 1990).

[11] AlphaStar Team, "AlphaStar: Mastering the Real-Time Strategy Game StarCraft II," DeepMind, https://deepmind.com/blog/article/alphastar -mastering-real-time-strategy-game-starcraft-ii.

[12] The key word here is *meaningful*. Whenever one suggests a test like this, somebody will try to find some way of gaming the test so that they can claim to have succeeded even if they do so in a way that you didn't anticipate. This is, of course, precisely what happened with the Turing test. What I'm after is programs that can do this in a substantive way—not programs that pass the test through a combination of smoke and mirrors.

[13] S. Baron-Cohen, A. M. Leslie, and U. Frith. "Does the Autistic Child Have a 'Theory of Mind'?," *Cognition* 21, no. 1 (1985): 37–46.

[14] Simon Baron-Cohen, *Mindblindness: An Essay on Autism and Theory of Mind* (Cambridge, MA: MIT Press, 1995).

[15] N. C. Rabinowitz et al. "Machine Theory of Mind," arXiv:1802.07740.

[16] I am no expert on evolutionary psychology: my guide in this section is Robin Dunbar's *Human Evolution* (New York: Penguin, 2014), and I am pleased to refer interested readers to this for more detail.

# Index

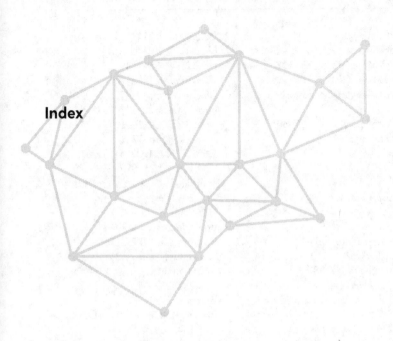